LECTURES

ON THE

INFLUENCE OF THE APOSTLE PAUL

ON THE

DEVELOPMENT OF CHRISTIANITY

AMS PRESS

NEW YORK

Library of Congress Cataloging in Publication Data

Pfleiderer, Otto, 1839-1908.
  Lectures on the influence of the Apostle Paul on the
development of Christianity.

  Reprint of the 1885 ed. published by Williams and
Norgate, London, which was issued as the 1885 Hibbert
lectures.
  1. Paul, Saint, apostle.   2. Bible.   N.T. Epistles
of Paul—Theology.   3. Theology, Doctrinal—History—
Early church, ca. 30-600.   I. Title.   II. Series:
Hibbert lectures (London); 1885.
BS2651.P4   1979   225.9'24   77-27166
ISBN 0-404-60406-4

First AMS edition published in 1979.

Reprinted from the edition of 1885, London. [Trim size and text
area of the original have been slightly altered in this edition.
Original trim size: 13.5 × 21 cm; text area: 9 × 15.3 cm.]

MANUFACTURED
IN THE UNITED STATES OF AMERICA

LECTURES

ON THE

INFLUENCE OF THE APOSTLE PAUL

ON THE

DEVELOPMENT OF CHRISTIANITY,

DELIVERED IN LONDON AND OXFORD,

IN APRIL AND MAY, 1885.

BY

OTTO PFLEIDERER, D.D.

PROFESSOR OF THEOLOGY IN THE UNIVERSITY OF BERLIN.

TRANSLATED BY J. FREDERICK SMITH.

WILLIAMS AND NORGATE,

14, HENRIETTA STREET, COVENT GARDEN, LONDON;
AND 20, SOUTH FREDERICK STREET, EDINBURGH.

1885.

LONDON:
PRINTED BY O. GREEN AND SON,
178, STRAND.

CONTENTS.

LECTURE III.

THE CONFLICT OF THE APOSTLE TO THE GENTILES WITH JEWISH CHRISTIANS.

LECTURE IV.

THE RECONCILIATION OF PAULINISM AND JEWISH CHRISTIANITY.

LECTURE V.

PAULINISM AND GNOSTICISM.

Lecture VI.

PAULINISM AND THE CHURCH.

Corrections.

Page 16, line 1, read "*by* Paul" for "*to* Paul."
Page 172, line 7, read "*complete* parallel" for "*direct* parallel."

LECTURE I.

THE FIRST CHURCH AND THE CONVERSION OF PAUL.

LECTURE I.

THE FIRST CHURCH AND THE CONVERSION
OF PAUL.

BEFORE I enter upon the subject of these Lectures, allow me to present to the Trustees of this Foundation my sincere and hearty thanks for the gratification which their invitation to undertake the delivery of the Hibbert Lectures for this year gave me. It was with mixed feelings, it is true, that I accepted the invitation. For much as I felt the honour and dignity put upon me by the request to continue the series of Lectures which have been delivered by such distinguished and famous men as the previous Hibbert Lecturers, the doubt weighed very heavily upon my mind whether I should be able to justify your confidence and to perform satisfactorily the task proposed to me. If it is no easy

thing to deal adequately in a few hours with such
a comprehensive and difficult subject as the significance of Paulinism in the development of Christianity confessedly is, in my case the difficulty is
increased by the fact that I am not fully master of
your language.   Though some twenty-two years ago
I spent a summer, which I can never forget, in your
country, and persuaded myself at the time that at
all events I understood English, such a period is
long enough to let one forget how to handle a foreign
language readily.   If, therefore, I have nevertheless ventured to accept your invitation, it has
been in the confident hope that you will kindly
take into account the special difficulties of the
foreigner addressing you, and that you will treat
the defects of his language and delivery with
forbearance.   I was induced, in spite of all these
doubts, to hazard the undertaking and meet the
wishes of the Trustees, not only by the pleasant
prospect of personally meeting old and new friends,
but especially by the attraction which the subject
itself has for me.   For the historical significance of
the Apostle Paul, his personality and doctrine, his

relation to Jesus and the First Church, no less than his influence on the development of Christianity in early and recent times, has always been to me one of the most interesting and important subjects of religious inquiry. It seems to me thus important from both doctrinal and practical points of view. For we have in it especially the key to an understanding of the origin and development of our religion; and a closer acquaintance with Paulinism—with its eternal religious truths and its perishable forms—might prove an excellent help towards the settlement of our religious troubles and the promotion of sound religious progress. On that account the treatment of this subject certainly falls within the range of the design of the Hibbert Trust, and I shall consider myself fortunate if I should succeed in contributing in a small degree by my Lectures to the furtherance of that truly grand and noble design.

Considering the importance of Paulinism in relation to Christianity, we might have expected that it would have long ago been thoroughly understood and elucidated by theologians, and that at all events.

complete agreement would have been arrived at
with regard to all chief points.   But a glance any-
where into the literature of the subject shows how
little this is the case at present.   We might almost
say that there is hardly another subject within the
whole range of ecclesiastical history with regard to
which opinions and conclusions so widely differ as
is the case with Paulinism.   This may be explained
in part by the special difficulties involved in the
subject itself, and in part by the fact that an unprejudiced historical examination of Paulinism is of
recent date, and has still to contend at every step
with the prepossessions of dogmatic sympathies or
antipathies.   As long as the Bible was read under
the suppositions involved in the orthodox doctrine
of inspiration, and nothing might be found in the
New Testament but the doctrinal system of a certain
theology, an eye for the peculiarities of the teaching
of Paul was altogether wanting: Paul was classed
together with the other biblical authors under the
ingenuous supposition that they all taught always
the same dogmatic truths, save that perhaps one did
this somewhat more plainly and at greater length

than the others. The Rationalism of the end of the latter and beginning of the present century, too, although it had emancipated itself from the fetters of the orthodox theory of inspiration, possessed too little historical perception to be able to appreciate even approximately the significance of Paul. It took offence at the dogmatical difficulties of the Pauline theology, and endeavoured more or less arbitrarily to soften them down, explain them away, or adjust them, and thereby of course deprived itself of the possibility of understanding the ideas of Paul in their own original significance and in accordance with their historical and psychological conditions. It was the strictly historical examination of primitive Christianity, as it originated with the great Tübingen theologian, Christian Ferdinand Baur, which first gave the key to an understanding of the characteristic peculiarities and the historical significance of the Apostle Paul. For it was that examination which, by an accurate critical sifting of the documents, proved how erroneous was the ancient tradition of the harmonious agreement of all the Apostles; how profound, on the contrary, was the antagonism between Paul and the first Apostles, how animated the contention of the parties, how protracted and laborious the process of their union in the Church.

By this means the way had undoubtedly been prepared for a proper appreciation of the historical significance of the Apostle Paul. But as so often happens in the course of human inquiry that newly-obtained knowledge is in the first instance exaggerated and unduly pressed, thereby giving rise to new errors, so was it in this instance. Even in the case of the earlier theologians of the so-called Tübingen School there was perceptible a certain inclination, in dwelling on the theological originality of the Apostle Paul, to put into the back-ground his religious dependence on Jesus in such a way that it might seem as if Christianity had proceeded really not from Jesus but from Paul. That was, indeed, never Baur's opinion : but in his pupil Schwegler's account of primitive Christianity an inference of this kind might undoubtedly seem to be implied. The inference has been subsequently made by others, and most distinctly by the philosopher Eduard von

Hartmann in his work on the *Entwickelung des religiösen Bewusstseins der Menschheit.*[1] According to von Hartmann, Paul, as "the inventor of Heathen Christianity and the dogma of Salvation," is alone entitled to be considered the author of the Christian Religion of Salvation, while, on the other hand, Jewish Christianity was in itself only "an eschatalogical dream" (*Schwärmerei*), like so many others, which would simply have figured amongst the curiosities of history if the credited facts about the death and resurrection of Jesus had not become in Paul's case the accidental occasion for basing on them an anti-Jewish universal religion. "If Paul had not invented Heathen Christianity, the idea would never have occurred to later ages that Jewish Christianity was anything else than a religion of Law peculiar to the Jewish nation, containing intensified Messianic expectations, and with a definite reference of those expectations to the person of a prophet who was not acknowledged while he lived and met with a violent death." That reference of the Messianic

---

[1] Pp. 525 sq.

expectation to the person of a prophet—in other
words, faith in the Messianic dignity of Jesus—is
regarded by von Hartmann as a personal addition
to the doctrines of Judaism, which leaves the sub-
stantial truths of the religion untouched: neither
Jesus, therefore, nor the First Church advanced in
religious principle beyond Judaism; the new principle of the universal Religion of Salvation originated
with the Apostle Paul.   There is some truth in
Hartmann's views.   It is true that the Messianic
movement would not have become the universal
religion of Christianity without the work of Paul.
But it has been forgotten that the work of Paul
presupposes as its indispensable basis the personal
history of Jesus, without which basis it would be as
a castle in the clouds.   The whole subject-matter of
the Epistles of Paul would be to us unintelligible,
the very fact of his change from a Pharisee into
an Apostle incomprehensible, and the success of his
missionary labours inexplicable, were we to throw
aside the one explanatory key which Paul himself
presents to us in the constantly recurring declaration:
" We preach not ourselves but Jesus Christ as the

Lord," and "I determined to know nothing among you save Jesus Christ the crucified one;" again, "Let a man account of us as servants of Christ and stewards of the mysteries of God;" or finally, "Other foundation can no man lay than that which is laid, which is Jesus Christ."[1] Simply to ignore these personal declarations of the Apostle would be in itself an unwarrantably arbitrary procedure, and is in the end rendered wholly impossible, as we shall see, by the fact that it is only by means of them that the history of Paul becomes intelligible. "The servant is not above his Lord"—we must accept that, and with it we reject at the commencement every attempt to exaggerate Paul's claims at the cost of Jesus as a mistake, the origin of which in von Hartmann's case may undoubtedly be discovered in the confusion of the Christian religion with Christian theology, a confusion which is always natural to the dominant intellectual bent of the philosopher. Christian theology, it is true, dates from Paul, but the Christian religion from Jesus, both his Lord and ours.

---

[1] 2 Cor. iv. 6 ; 1 Cor. iv. 1, iii. 11, ii. 2.

Yet this very fact that Paul was the originator of Christian theology—of the full exposition and development in a didactic and doctrinal form of the Christian consciousness—has, again, given rise to an estimate of the Apostle's influence, the opposite of that just discussed. From several quarters Paul is charged with having disfigured the simple "Christianity of Christ" by his dogmatic speculations. While the gospel of Jesus, it is said—those beautiful ethical truths of the Sermon on the Mount, for instance—is plain and attractive to everybody, Paul, with his doctrine of Christ's person and atonement, has, on the contrary, introduced into Christianity that element of the supernatural, with much that is above and contrary to reason, which imposes on the reason a heavier cross than all the works of the Law ever were. Instead of bringing liberty, it is complained, there is thus due to him with his dogmas a new and the worst bondage of the human mind. But this estimate is even, if possible, less historical and more shallow in its depreciation of Paul than the former was in its exaggeration of his importance. It is undoubtedly true that the Chris-

tian spirit which was still in Jesus the direct life
of prophetic genius, had in Paul been already cast
in the technical forms of doctrine and dogma. It
is true also that, in the construction of the Pauline
doctrinal system, various elements of the thought of
the time were employed, and elements which cannot
all lay claim to validity for all time, and in which
the specific idea of Christianity has not yet found
its pure expression. But are we on that account
justified in concluding that those dogmatic forms
were altogether unnecessary, and that without them
Christianity could have become the religion of the
world, and an established ecclesiastical institution,
or could have survived amidst the commotions of
time? Is it conceivable that the ideal spirit of
the gospel of Jesus would ever have succeeded in
emancipating itself from massive Judean particularism, which even in the First Church presented
such stout resistance to it, unless Paul, the former
Pharisee and Scribe, had risen above the Law
through the Law, and had got the victory over
Judaism by the aid of its own weapons, which he
took from the armoury of Rabbinism itself? How

can we imagine that the crucified Messiah of the Jews could have made his triumphant march through the Greek and Roman world, if he had not put on, in Paul's proclamation of him, the luminous form of the celestial Son of God, in which also he could be readily received by the religious and philosophical consciousness of the Heathen world? If we must deny the possibility of that, we have obviously no right to censure the Apostle for accomplishing his divinely great task with the aid of the human means the time supplied. Does he not himself say, "We have this treasure in earthen vessels, that the exceeding greatness of the power may be of God and not from us"?[1] He thereby justifies us in distinguishing in his teaching between the precious treasure, which consists of the divine and saving power of the gospel, and the earthen vessel—that is, his dogmatic forms of teaching, containing the treasure. In fact, it is just here that the real problem of a scientific examination of Paulinism presents itself. That problem is especially to show how Paul, as

---

[1] 2 Cor. iv. 7.

more powerfully affected by the spirit of Jesus than any one else, sought on his part, by means of the conceptions of his age, to apprehend and comprehend that spirit, how he brought the conceptions of Pharisaism especially into the service of the new truth, and thereby subjected them to a transformation, the result of which was the new and magnificent religious system of the founder of Christian theology.

As in mountainous regions the real height of the loftiest summits is not perceptible close at hand, but can be observed only by the more distant spectator, so in human history it is of very common occurrence that the full significance of the principal personages is much less clearly perceived in their immediate neighbourhood than at a greater distance : it is to those further removed only that the full characteristic image of such personages is presented plainly, while to those closer at hand the larger total impression is often lost sight of behind the small impressions of every-day intercourse. Just this occurred also in the relation of Jesus to the first Apostles and to Paul. Paradoxical as it may seem

that to Paul, who had never listened to the words
of Jesus, the inmost *spirit* of Jesus should have been
more purely and profoundly apprehended than by
the original disciples, such a thing is not incomprehensible.   The nature of that spirit had been
revealed to him from the very first in the concen-
trated light of the focus of the great act of his life,
in the light of his death on the cross ; and from that
point of view he perceived in him the end of the
ancient religion of the letter which killeth and the
beginning of the new religion of the life-giving spirit
of adoption and love.   Thus Paul perceived more
profoundly and brought out more distinctly than the
other disciples what was original in Jesus, the divine
genius of his personality, wherein precisely lay his
vocation to be the Saviour of the world.

Undoubtedly the other disciples had, under the
impression produced by their daily intercourse with
Jesus, been so powerfully affected by him, that their
faith in him and his divine mission was strong
enough even to survive and to overcome that which
was so paradoxical to them in the course of his
history.   Inasmuch as the gospel of the kingdom of

God, which had given them such deep satisfaction, could not be a delusion, the Man of God, who was destined to bring that kingdom to his people, could not have gone away for ever, but must be given to them again that he might triumphantly finish his work. This postulate of their faith, this hope of their love, which was stronger than death, became to them the certainty of sight in the experiences of the first Easter; for the miraculous Christophanies, which were shared at times by individuals and at times by many at once in the exalted moments of their common religious exercises, were regarded by them as the prelude and pledge of the near return of their Lord for the permanent establishment of his kingdom. From that time forth their hope and longing were directed to that return; their faith in the Messianic dignity of Jesus reached its climax in the expectation of his immediate second coming. But since elsewhere in the Jewish nation of that time a belief in the speedy coming of the Messiah prevailed, the faith of the earliest Church of the disciples of Jesus differed, when strictly looked at, from that of the rest of the Jews simply in this, that the former

hoped to behold again in the Messiah, whose coming
all expected, the crucified Jesus, whom the latter
abhorred as a criminal. It is true this *one* point
of difference concealed within it a profound chasm,
which required only to be realized and thought out
in its consequences, to conduct to a complete separation between the Church of the disciples of Jesus and
Judaism. But this is just what did not take place
within the primitive Church. On the contrary, in
its thought and feeling, that point of difference was
outweighed by what it possessed in common with
Judaism; and that common possession was not merely
the general dogmatic axioms, but particularly the
view of the Messianic kingdom as the terrestrial
consummation of the national Judean theocracy on
the basis of the perpetuated Mosaic Law.

In the view of impartial historical inquiry, no
doubt exists as to the point, that the earliest Christians were still very far from conceiving the kingdom of Christ as a spiritual kingdom of truth and
godliness, or even of celestial blessedness. *We* may
be tempted to interpret some of the descriptions of
the kingdom of Christ found in the New Testament

as mere symbols of spiritual truths, but we have no right whatever to ascribe this interpretation to the earliest Christians, as if they in their time had intended such ideas of the Messianic kingdom to be understood as merely symbolical representations and not quite seriously in their literal sense. This is the case when in the Gospels the expectation is presented in the form of a promise of Jesus that in the Messianic kingdom the Apostles will sit on twelve thrones and judge the twelve tribes of Israel; that they will receive again, as a reward for their present sacrifices, all that they have lost, including lands and houses, a hundred-fold; that they will recline at table with patriarchs and drink of the fruit of the vine.[1] It is the case also when the Apocalypse describes the new Jerusalem as a royal city, glistening with gold and jewels, coming down from heaven to the earth, and sees the names of the twelve Apostles written on its foundation-stones; or when disciples of the Apostles, of the second century, such as Papias, give descriptions, with genuine

---

[1] Matt. xix. 28, 29, viii. 11, xxvi. 29.

Oriental imagination, of the gigantic vines of the kingdom of God.

With regard to the national Jewish character of the kingdom of the Messiah, too, the conception of the earliest Christians accorded substantially with that of the rest of the Jewish nation.   It is the kingdom of Israel as to the restoration of which, according to the Acts, the Apostles interrogate the Lord at his ascension; to the children of the prophets, and of the covenant of the fathers of Israel, the kingdom is assigned, as Peter says;[1] and, according to the Apocalypse, the number of the tribes of Israel determines the measure of the new Jerusalem. Though individual conversions of Heathen might occur, they could not really affect the essentially Jewish character of the Messianic community, such conversions having been, in fact, anticipated by the prophets as taking place in the Messianic age.   The First Church was far from thinking of the conversion of the masses of the Heathen, or of a regularly constituted mission to them.   In fact, the return of

---

[1] Acts i. 6, iii. 25.

the Lord was believed to be so near, that there
would not be sufficient time to proclaim the gospel
message throughout the cities of Israel even.[1] Moreover, Jesus was said to have expressly forbidden
his disciples to extend their missionary labours
beyond Israel : " Go ye not into the way of the
Gentiles nor into a city of the Samaritans, but go
rather to the lost sheep of the house of Israel."[2]
It may, it is true, be conjectured that this utterance
did not in its present definite form originate before
the time when, in consequence of the appearance of
Paul on the scene, the question of the mission to
the Heathen had become a subject of animated
controversy in the First Church ; but it could not
well have been quoted as a saying of Jesus if opposite utterances, such as the command to preach to
the Heathen, Matt. xxviii. 19, had been remem-
bered. Whatever may be the exact truth with
regard to these and similar utterances of Jesus, in
any case, according to the concurrent tradition of
the Gospels, it is certain that Jesus himself confined

---

[1] Matt. x. 23.   [2] Matt. x. 5.

his Messianic labours to Israel alone, and did not contemplate their extension to the Heathen world. So far the First Church could appeal to the example of Jesus, whilst the Pauline universalism was involved as the corollary and outcome of the spirit of Jesus, as it is expressed in the saying, that God causes His sun to shine on the just and the unjust.

As the First Church could not conceive the Messianic kingdom otherwise than within the framework of the national Jewish theocracy, the case was the same with regard to the perpetual validity of the Mosaic Law.   The first Christians lived and moved completely within the prescribed forms of Jewish piety, frequented the Temple, observed the hours of prayer, the fasts, the festivals, the laws regarding food, the customary vows, with a conscientiousness which placed their loyalty to the Law, even in the eyes of the Jewish people, beyond all doubt, and enabled them to appear really as "zealots for the Law," that is, as Jews of the strictest party.[1] Though now and again individuals, like Peter in

---

[1] Acts ii. 46, 47, v. 13, xxi. 20.

the case of Cornelius, and subsequently in Antioch,
might on an occasion rise superior to the letter
of the Law, and in this practical exhibition of
liberal feeling betray some effects of the previous
freer spirit of Jesus, that was far from a conscious
emancipation on principle from the Law. Of such
an emancipation no mention could be made in the
First Church, for the simple reason that the question
as to the permanent validity of the Law had evidently not come within the horizon of that Church
prior to the missionary labours of Paul. The Church
supposed as a simple matter of course that the
Messianic community which looked for the speedy
fulfilment of the promises made to the Fathers,
would necessarily be based on the foundation of the
Law of God given to the Fathers; no one in the
First Church had conceived the possibility of a
Messianic community apart from this basis of the
Jewish Law. But when subsequently, in consequence of the Pauline mission, the question was
proposed practically, whether Heathen believers
might be regarded as Christian brethren without
first becoming Jews, through the energetic action

of Paul and the valuable assistance of Peter, a decision in favour of the dispensation of Heathen Christians from the Law was successfully adopted, but in the case of Jewish Christians it was determined that, just as before, the obligatory character of the Law should remain intact. Nor did the Jewish-Christian Church subsequently ever get beyond this boundary-line; on the contrary, it afterwards sought to retract the concession of freedom in favour of the Heathen. All the long and violent conflicts which Paul had subsequently to wage with Jewish Christianity in connection with the question of the Law, would be unintelligible on the supposition that the First Church was from the commencement of the same way of thinking as Paul with regard to the dispensation of Christians from the Law; they constitute therefore an irrefragable proof that the First Church considered itself perpetually subject to the Jewish Law.

We shall, moreover, find this Judaic conservatism of the earliest Christians the more intelligible and excusable if we recollect that in this respect also they simply held by the example of Jesus, who with

all the inward freedom of his heart and soul in
relation to matters of the Law, at the same time
submitted himself in his outward actions to all the
existing customs and institutions of his nation.
When the Master had said, that he had come not to
destroy but to fulfil, how could the disciples think
of destroying? It is true that the first disciples of
Jesus, perhaps even Jesus himself, had not clearly
perceived that the fulfilment of the Divine will,
when conceived with such profound spirituality as
it was by Jesus—that is, in the sense of a divine
and absolute goodness and purity of heart—of itself
involves the invalidating of the unspiritual ritual
and ceremonial Law, and therefore in its consequences the abrogation of it in the course of time.
They had probably learnt, in their intercourse with
Jesus, that mercy is more than sacrifices and keeping
the Sabbath, purity of heart more than washing of
hands and straining out gnats; but they had so
accustomed themselves to regard ethical virtues as
secondary to ceremonial observances and as their harmonious completion, that they had no feeling for the
profound antagonism of principle existing between

them.   The antithesis between Law and Gospel,
which the Pharisee Paul afterwards so pointedly
recognized that from the beginning there was for
him simply the alternative, either a Christian or a
Jew, had never been so distinctly perceived by the
earlier Apostles as to put before them the alternative of loyalty to the Law or faith in Christ.   That,
therefore, which seemed to be, and in a certain
respect really was, the advantage of the earlier
Apostles over Paul—their regular education by
means of personal intercourse with Jesus, which
also gradually reconciled the differences between
the old and the new principle—was the very thing
that, to a certain extent, proved their disadvantage, in as far as it veiled from their view the
new and anti - Judaic principle in the work of
Jesus.   Inasmuch as the antagonism between the
old and the new religion had never been quite
clearly perceived by them during the life of Jesus,
his death could not afterwards open their eyes to it.
Their faith endeavoured to get over the offence of
the cross as quickly as possible, endeavoured to
minimize, to excuse, to put another construction on

this scandal to a Jewish mind; and precisely this kept them from entering so unreservedly into the significance of that offensive fact as to be able to fully realize the momentous importance of its consequences. They looked upon the death of Jesus as the martyrdom of the Righteous One, of which human ignorance had been the sinful cause, and which God had permitted, and to which certainly, according to the words of the prophet (Isaiah liii.) concerning the suffering Servant of God, a salutary virtue for the forgiveness of sins was to be ascribed, as the Jewish theologians generally maintained with regard to all the sufferings of a righteous man. But the view of the Apostle Paul—that Christ's death, in which the Holy One succumbed to the curse of the Law, signified the final abrogation of the Law of the letter—was wholly unknown to the First Church. In its view, the death of the Messiah was only a further supplementary means of salvation in addition to the ancient means and works of the Law, while for Paul it was the new means of salvation *in the place of* the entire ancient legal system. In the view of the first Christians, Jesus was, and remained, *notwithstanding* his death on the cross, the Messiah of the Jews; but in Paul's view he became the Saviour of the world *by virtue of* that ignominious death.

As long as the Apostolic Church exhibited this conservative attitude towards the Jewish Law, no serious conflicts between it and the Jewish authorities could arise. Though its proclamation of the resurrection and Messiahship of the crucified Jesus might be obnoxious to the heads of the nation, there was no ground for an energetic employment of force against it, as the disciples of Jesus displayed in their conduct such a blameless loyalty to the Law that they enjoyed amongst the people the reputation of exemplary piety. These devout believers in their Messiah, it was at first thought in the circles of the Pharisees, might be let alone as harmless enthusiasts, inasmuch as they were really in other respects as good Jews as could be. The well-known counsel of Gamaliel was in fact the most sagacious that could, from the Jewish standpoint, be given with regard to the Messianic movement. If this peaceable relation had been kept up, without doubt the Messianic movement would never have grown beyond the limits of a Jewish sect, and as such would have expired, at all events, with the destruction of Jerusalem; Christ would then have died in vain, since his spirit and life-work would have been extinguished in the restrictions of Judaism. For the future of Christianity it was therefore of decisive moment that the bolder action of the Hellenist Stephen interrupted the tranquil life of the infant Church in Jerusalem, and set rolling the stone which from that time forth no human power could stop.

It was probably no accident that this new impetus originated with a Hellenist and not a Hebrew. The Hellenistic Jews had, in consequence of their contact with Heathen culture, in various other respects obtained greater freedom of view, and adhered less tenaciously than the Jews of Palestine to the Temple services and other ceremonial observances, above which they ranked the ethical portions of the Law. In fact, Philo even found it necessary to oppose rationalistic Jews of this description belonging to the Diaspora, who supposed it allow-

able to let go the letter of the Law in their attention to its spiritual meaning. If, therefore, an
Hellenist with these more liberal views had become
acquainted with Jesus in his last days in Jerusalem,
for instance, and had witnessed his rejection by the
hierarchy, how easily might it then have happened
that the powerful denunciations uttered by Jesus
against the empty formality of the official theologians
should touch a responsive chord in his heart, and
stir thoughts in which the mind of Jesus would find
truer expression than in the conservative Jewish
Christianity of the Hebrew early Church! Whatever may be the exact literal fact with regard to
the accusation raised against both Stephen and
Jesus of having blasphemed the Temple, the very
circumstance that tradition has preserved both accu-
sations in nearly the same forms, betrays unmistakable traces of the close connection which existed
between the reformatory labours of Jesus and the
action of Stephen. It is not without significance,
therefore, that the Church placed the festival of the
protomartyr Stephen immediately after the birthday
of Jesus, for it was really he who saved the life-

work of Jesus from stagnation in Jewish tradition-
alism, inasmuch as he was the first to bring out the
profound difference between the crucified Son of
Man and legal Judaism, becoming thereby the historical link between Jesus and Paul.

On the occasion of the tumultuous trial in which
the first martyr of the infant Church fell a sacrifice,
the Pharisee and Scribe, Paul of Tarsus, took a
prominent part as an eager opponent of the Christians. He was the witness at whose feet the execu-
tioners of Stephen laid their garments; he was then
the confidential ally of the Sanhedrin, who was sent
to Damascus with large discretionary powers for the
further persecution of the fugitives. But the man
that had set out for the persecution of the Christians
arrived in Damascus a convert. What was it which
effected this sudden change in the fanatical Pharisee
and zealot of the Law? There are, as we know, in
the Acts of the Apostles three separate accounts[1] of
the conversion of Paul, between which there is so
much difference that none of them can be regarded

---

[1] Acts ix. xxiv. and xxvi.

as an accurate historical description; yet they appear
to possess as their common nucleus the fact that his
conversion was the effect of a sudden event of an
extraordinary character, which was attended by a
violent mental and physical convulsion of the whole
man, during which he believed he saw and heard a
revelation of the Messiah Jesus. And therewith the
direct declarations of Paul himself in his Epistles
are in agreement, the decisive experience appearing,
according to them, likewise to have consisted of a
Christophany. When he asks, 1 Cor. ix. 1, for
instance, "Have not I seen the Lord Jesus Christ?"
according to the context the words can only refer to
a sight of Christ of such a nature as established the
apostolic dignity of Paul, and must accordingly have
been connected with his call to be an Apostle at his
conversion. And when, after recounting the previous appearances of Christ, 1 Cor. xv. 9, he continues, "Last of all he appeared to me also as to an
untimely birth, for I am the least of the Apostles,
who am not worthy to be called an Apostle, because
I persecuted the Church; but through the grace of
God I am what I am," it is clear that in this pas-

sage also he traces his call to the Apostleship to an appearing of Christ, which he ranks, as essentially similar, with the earlier appearances of the risen Lord. It is accordingly beyond doubt that Paul was fully convinced of the objective reality of the appearance of Christ with which he was favoured; at the same time, however, he seems elsewhere to intimate that it was not an ordinary seeing and hearing with the physical senses, but an inward experience within his soul. For he says, with evident reference to his conversion, Gal. i. 16, "It pleased God to reveal his Son *in me*, that I might preach him among the Heathen;" and 2 Cor. iv. 6, "God shined *in our hearts* for the illumination of the knowledge of the glory of God in the face of Jesus Christ." But in that case we shall be justified in placing the event on the road to Damascus in the same category with those other "visions and revelations" of which Paul elsewhere often speaks[1]—that is, it is allowable to place that decisive experience, notwithstanding its extraordinary character, in the category of visions,

---

[1] 2 Cor. xii. 1 sq.; Gal. ii. 2; comp. Acts xvi. 9, xxvii. 23.

which are at all events to a certain degree to be explained from the mental condition of the subject.[1] Moreover, those who look upon the conversion of Paul as a miracle in the strictest sense of the word, are unable, nevertheless, to dispense altogether with a psychological preparation for it, inasmuch as otherwise the conversion would have to be regarded as a direct and immediate, that is magical, act of God, in which the soul of Paul would have succumbed to an alien force, which would be a view wholly opposed to the genius of Christianity, and in direct contradiction to the Apostle's own definition of faith as an act of moral obedience.

We possess in the words which the Acts of the Apostles (xxvi. 14) represents Paul as hearing from the lips of Jesus, "It is hard for thee to kick against the goad," a hint for the psychological explanation

---

[1] It is true that this would not be possible according to the account of the Acts, because in it the marvellous appearance is witnessed not by Paul alone, but also by his attendants. But it appears plainly merely from the discrepancies between the various accounts of the Acts, that that circumstance cannot be regarded as historical, but must be ascribed to the influence of embellishing tradition.

of the change. Before his conversion, accordingly, Paul had felt a goad in his soul, against which he vainly sought to kick. In what else can it have consisted than in the painful doubt as to the lawfulness of his persecution of the Christians—in the doubt, therefore, whether the truth was really on his side, and not rather, after all, on that of the persecuted disciples of Christ? But how was it possible that a doubt like this should arise in the soul of the fanatical Pharisee? The occasion for this had been just then supplied by his participation in the persecution of the Christians. The very sight of the joyful martyrs' courage with which the Christians met suffering and death for the name of their crucified Lord, necessarily affected powerfully the tender soul of Paul, and pressed upon him the question, whether men who could die so gladly for their faith could really be blasphemers; whether a faith which produced such heroism could be a delusion. But we must consider, in addition, that on such occasions Paul could not avoid hearing the defence made by the Christians, and therefore being made acquainted with the proofs of the truth of their faith and taking them into consideration. When, in reply to their apologies, he maintained that he who had been rejected by his own nation could not possibly be the Messiah of that nation, they answered him that it was written in the Scriptures themselves, "The stone which the builders had rejected was destined to become the corner-stone." If he urged further, "Cursed is every one that hangeth on a tree," the crucified Jesus died under the curse of God, they met him with the passage of Isaiah in which there is said of the Servant of God, "Surely he hath borne our sicknesses and took upon himself our pains, was wounded for our transgressions and smitten for our sins; the punishment was laid on him that we might have peace, and by his wounds we are healed." And that this significance of the death of Jesus as a vicarious means of propitiation did not fail to produce an impression on the Pharisee Paul, is in the highest degree probable, inasmuch as it certainly fell in with the prevailing view of the theology of the Pharisees, in which the unmerited sufferings of the righteous generally were regarded as an atonement for the sins of their families and

their nation.   This theory, it is true, had not been
in the theology of the Pharisees applied to the
Messiah, because the feature of bearing and suffering generally did not find a place in their ideal of
the Messiah.   But after the Christians had once
given to the passage of Isaiah the Messianic interpretation, no valid objection could be brought
against it from the Pharisaic standpoint.   Indeed,
we may go further and say, that when once the
Pharisee considered and thought out in its consequences, in the first instance only as a hypothesis,
the idea of the vicarious propitiatory suffering of
the Messiah, from that point of view the solution of
a difficulty might offer itself under which his faith
in other respects painfully suffered.   That is, the
Pharisees expected the coming of the Messiah in the
immediate future for the deliverance of his people,
while all the time it was no less one of their established beliefs that the days of the Messiah would
be beheld only by a righteous nation.   Where, then,
was this righteous nation, completely answering to
the Divine will?   Had, then, all the convulsive
efforts of the Pharisees to lead the nation to right-

eousness produced any effect at all? Did they not
condemn themselves in their bitter contempt of the
masses who knew nothing of the Law? Indeed,
was not the conscientious Pharisee obliged to confess
that he had never been able in his own case even
to attain the ideal of righteousness to which he had
aspired—that all his zeal for righteousness had failed
to conquer, but had rather provoked and increased,
the resistance of his sinful desires? We may safely
infer from Paul's subsequent description of the
inward conflict in man,[1] that he himself as a Pharisee had really passed through and painfully suffered
under such experiences. The question might therefore the more naturally force itself upon him and
occupy his mind, whether, inasmuch as the righteousness of the Messianic kingdom cannot be attained by our own efforts, it was not meant to be
accomplished by the Messiah himself. Was it not
therefore meant to be not so much the condition of
his coming as rather the effect and object of it?
Was not, perhaps, precisely the undeserved suffering

---

[1] Rom. vii. 12 sq.

of such a righteous servant of God as Jesus must have been, according to the delineations of his disciples, intended to be the divinely ordered means of rendering sinners righteous before God?

The more Paul considered such thoughts as these, the less could he help perceiving that the faith of the Christians in the Messianic dignity of the crucified Jesus was after all not so foolish and wicked as he had at first supposed; that, on the contrary, the possibility of the truth of that faith could be denied off-hand least of all from the standpoint of beliefs held by the Pharisees. But if he had only once been compelled to allow this possibility, the justice of his persecution of the Christian Church had been rendered doubtful. How heavily must this doubt weigh upon the tender conscience of Paul! If previously, in the excitement and commotion of action in Jerusalem, he succeeded in getting rid of his doubts, now on the lonely road to Damascus they would the more irresistibly assail him, and penetrate as goads his soul. How will he have prayed for a solution of the enigma, for a satisfaction of his doubt! That

the crucified Jesus might be the Messiah was shown
by the Scriptures; but by what sign should Paul
know that he *really* was the Messiah? The faith
of the disciples was based on the fact that they had
seen Jesus as the risen Lord who had been raised
to God's right hand; and Paul could perceive by
the glorified countenance of the dying Stephen how
sacred that conviction was to them. Could this
conviction be a lie or a delusion? But if it was
true, *then*—such must have been Paul's inference—
God Himself had taken the side of the Crucified
One and by an unparalleled miracle declared him
to be the Messiah, not merely in the Jewish sense
of the Son of David, but in the much higher sense
of the celestial Son of God; *then* the death of
Jesus was consequently the undeserved death of
the Son of God for the propitiation of our sins; *then*
faith in him was the divinely ordained means of
justification; *then* satisfaction was provided for the
hitherto hopeless longing of his heart for peace with
God. Thus in this crucial moment for the Pharisee
Paul, everything, life or death, salvation or ruin,
depended on the one question, whether the crucified

Jesus had been in reality exalted by God to be the celestial Messiah.

Whilst his contending thoughts were being agitated concerning this crucial point, the image of the crucified Jesus, as Stephen had seen it at his death, presented itself with increasing distinctness prominently before Paul's inward vision. Though that image might be very unlike the Pharisaic ideal of the Messiah, it had, nevertheless, unmistakable points of kinship with ideal creations of the Jewish and Hellenistic speculation, which were well known to the theologian Paul. In Jewish Apocalyptic writings, ever since Daniel, a Son of Man had been spoken of, who would come to judge the world in the clouds of heaven.[1] Jewish and Hellenistic theology spoke of an archetypal Man in heaven, as the copy of whom Adam had been created;[2] it spoke also of a divine Wisdom and a divine Word, which had been independent organs

---

[1] Dan. vii. 13.

[2] Phil. *Leg. Allegor.* I. 12 (Mang. I. p. 49); *De Mundi Opif.* 46 (Mang. I. p. 32).

and mediators of God in the creation and government of the world, in sacred history especially the
organs of revelation.[1] Conceptions of this kind, the
relation of which to each other and to the Messianic
idea was still very vague and variable, might on
that very account be the more easily connected in
the mind of Paul with the image of the risen Jesus,
which agitated his soul in the midst of its doubts.
Thus everything combined to procure an increas-
ingly definite form and constantly deeper hold for
that image in the soul of the persecuting Pharisee.
Whilst he was still advancing on the road to per-
secute Jesus in his disciples, Jesus had so profoundly
and irresistibly, in the form in which he lived in
the minds of his disciples, taken possession of the
soul of Paul, that all the resistance of the Pharisee
was of no avail.

Do we, therefore, still need a miracle to explain
the decisive event, that sight of the celestial Christ,
which assisted in bringing Paul's faith into full and

---

[1] Prov. viii. 22 sq.; Sirach xxiv.; Baruch iii.; Enoch xlii. 2;
Wisdom of Sol. vii. 22 sq.; Philo, *passim*.

conscious existence? It appears to me that we are in a position to perceive fully the mental condition and circumstances from which the *vision* of Paul can be psychologically explained : an excitable, nervous temperament, a soul which had been violently agitated and torn by the most terrible doubts; a most vivid phantasy, occupied with the awful scenes of persecution on the one hand, and on the other by the ideal image of the celestial Christ; in addition, the nearness of Damascus with the urgency of a decision, the lonely stillness, the scorching and blinding heat of the desert—in fact, everything combined to produce one of those ecstatic states in which the soul believes that it sees those images and conceptions which profoundly agitate it, as if they were phenomena proceeding from the outward world. However, whether we are satisfied with this psychologically explained vision, or prefer to regard an objective Christophany in addition necessary to explain the conversion of Paul, it remains in either case certain that it was God who in the soul of Paul caused a light to shine to give the light of the knowledge of the glory of God in the face of

Jesus Christ.[1]   How, with this light, a new world
of faith and life arose upon the Apostle, we shall
have to see in our next Lecture.

---

[1] 2 Cor. iv. 6.

LECTURE II.

THE DOCTRINAL TEACHING OF PAUL.

THE DOCTRINAL TEACHING OF PAUL.

THE theology of the Apostle Paul is the development, on the basis of the previous beliefs of his Jewish theology, of that faith in Christ which became a certainty to him at his conversion. Jewish theology supplied the material in which his Christian teaching found its expression. But that material underwent a thorough-going reconstruction under the influence of the new spirit which pervaded it; it became the receptacle for the new energies of religious life which the Apostle received with his faith in Christ. The theology of Paul did not originate in his head, was not the product of cold ratiocination, but had its source in the heart, in the living experience of that power of God to effect salvation which the Gospel brings with it. But Paul's was a richly-endowed nature, in which the necessity of distinctness of knowledge and the power of consecutive thought were not less strong than the depth and warmth of his emotion. On that account Paul had no rest until he had brought the new conviction which had come to him outside Damascus into intimate relation with his previous convictions, had subordinated all details to this fresh centre, and had thus formed a new system of theological doctrine. Hence arose likewise the two-fold aspect which this theology has always presented to its students : on the one hand, it appears to resemble an ingenious scholastic system, which produces upon us a repulsive impression, the material of its conceptions having been taken from Jewish modes of thought ; while, on the other hand, it is evidently the expression of the deepest and strongest religious life, the embodiment of the loftiest moral ideal, and the symbol of those inmost experiences of the heart which constitute the essence of the Christian Religion of Salvation.

Was the crucified Jesus really the risen Christ

and Lord from heaven? This was the question at issue in the conflicts in Paul's soul preparatory to his conversion. As soon as this question had been set at rest by the vision of Christ, the fundamental principle of his gospel was settled in his mind. The very thing that had previously been to him the stone of stumbling and offence, then became the foundation and corner - stone of his new religious system. Thenceforth he determined to know nothing but Jesus Christ as the crucified and risen Lord. These two facts (which in his view become one, in so far as it was precisely by his resurrection that the crucified Jesus was shown to be the Christ and the saving significance of his death on the cross was guaranteed) constituted the Alpha and Omega of his gospel, whilst nothing else—not even the life of Jesus on the earth—was taken into consideration at all. For the very reason that he had become convinced of this cardinal point by an inward process, Paul could say,[1] that he had not received or learnt his gospel

---

[1] Gal. i. 12, 15, 16.

E

from men, but by revelation of Jesus Christ; for when it pleased God to reveal his Son in him, he did not confer with flesh and blood, did not even go up to Jerusalem to the older Apostles, but retired into Arabia, and not until three years afterwards did he have intercourse with Peter, on a visit of fourteen days to Jerusalem. If we may suppose that Paul used this three years' retreat into Arabia after his conversion for the purpose of thinking over, making his own, and shaping the new conviction at which he had arrived, it follows that his gospel had already been fixed in his mind when he sought to make the acquaintance of the older Apostles. The historical information which he may have gathered from Peter on that occasion he passes over with significant silence, which indicates plainly enough of how little moment that information was as regards his line of Christian thought, which had already been settled.

This declaration of the Apostle has been variously called in question, or at all events attempts have been made to qualify it. But we are not at all justified in so doing, since every inspection of the Pauline

Epistles confirms its absolute correctness. The gospel which Paul expounds in this passage is in fact exactly what we should expect from his description of its origin. It is nothing else than "the word of the Cross," that is, the proclamation of the crucified and risen Christ Jesus with the religious and moral inferences involved therein. Isolated references to utterances of Jesus, it is true, occur, which presuppose a certain acquaintance with the gospel tradition. But most of them are of entirely secondary significance; the account of the institution of the Lord's Supper only is of greater importance; but it is just in this case that Paul appears, when we look more closely, not to appeal to a human transmission of historical information, but to a direct revelation of Christ,[1] a view which is in complete accord with the fact that his version of the words used by Jesus on the institution of the rite presents a dogmatic turn which differs from the older gospel tradition, and of which he may very

---

[1] 1 Cor. xi. 23, Ἐγὼ γὰρ παρέλαβον ἀπὸ τοῦ κυρίου; comp. Gal. i. 12.

well have become convinced by the inward process
of religious induction.   To this must be added
the negative consideration, that just in those cases
in which Paul had the most direct and urgent
occasion to appeal to utterances of Jesus, or to the
example of his earthly life, he never does this: for
instance, when he is dealing with the worthless-
ness of the ceremonial Law for Christians, or with
love as the true fulfilling of the Law, or with examples of humility and willing self-sacrifice; in which
last case, it is true, Paul refers to Christ,[1] not,
however, to the extremely relevant example of his
earthly life, but to his incarnation, and accordingly
to considerations taken not from history, but from
dogmatic speculation.   In all this lies a distinct
confirmation of what Paul himself testifies regarding
the origin of his gospel: that he had not received it
by human tradition, but by the revelation of Christ;
that is, that it was based, not upon an intimate
knowledge of the outward life of Jesus, but upon
an inward vision of the spiritual nature of Christ,

---

[1] 2 Cor. viii. 9 ; Phil. ii. 5 sq.

and therefore upon the spontaneous rise of religious intuitions, which remained, however, all along connected with the historical person of Jesus by means of the one fact of the crucifixion. On this very account, that in the faith of Paul all salvation proceeded from this one point of the *death* of Jesus, everything else, including even the earthly *life* of Jesus, might well appear to him as insignificant. "Henceforth," he says (2 Cor. v. 16), "know we no man after the flesh; though we have known Christ after the flesh, henceforth know we him no more; therefore if any man is in Christ, he is a new creature; old things are passed away; behold, they are become new!" Looking upon himself, therefore, as in Christ a new man, on whom a new world of the spirit has arisen, everything which belongs to the old natural sphere of existence loses all religious significance; for this reason he is now also determined "to know nothing of Christ after the flesh," that is, of the earthly appearance and manner of life of Jesus as the Son of David after the flesh, but henceforth he knows Christ only as the Son of God after the spirit, as the Lord who is the Spirit and the Man from

heaven.[1]   Undoubtedly this was magnificently daring idealism, and the very thing which was required
to liberate Christianity from its Jewish fetters; but
with all its exaltation above the external phenomena
of history, this ideal conception of Christ is at the
same time the true representation of the *spirit* of
Jesus when freed from all earthly elements, the
mirror of his divine glory, as it was brightly reflected
in the pure and noble soul of the Apostle.

If we now examine somewhat more closely this
Pauline conception of Christ, we shall find that it
corresponds, feature by feature, to what has been
just said with regard to its origin.   As a light
from heaven, Paul had seen Christ near Damascus.
According to the Biblical conception, light is everywhere the form in which spirit generally and the
spirits manifest themselves, just as heaven is their
place of abode.   When Christ, therefore, was beheld
as a luminous appearance coming from heaven,
he appeared to be a celestial spirit in whom the
nature of God was imaged forth.   He is therefore
called the image of God, the Son of God, God's

---

[1] Rom. i. 3, 4 ; 2 Cor. iii. 17 ; 1 Cor. xv. 47.

own and first-born Son, in whom God loves his
own and most closely related image and likeness,
and on whose face the light of the glory of God
is reflected.[1]   Inasmuch as he is " the spirit "
absolutely in an entirely unique manner, the attributes peculiar to spirit likewise belong to him in a
unique way: he is holy spirit, untouched by sin;
and he is quickening spirit, the organ of God even
in the first creation,[2] and then, again, in the new
creation or resurrection, of which he is the beginning and archetype. For that reason he is called
also " the Lord" absolutely, the name which is in
the Old Testament given to God only. By such
conceptions Christ is brought so near to God that we
need feel no surprise when Paul at length calls
him without reserve, " God who is over all," in order
thereby to indicate his pre-eminent dignity and
dominion.[3]   At the same time, the Old Testament

---

[1] 2 Cor. iv. 4, 6 ; Rom. i. 4, viii. 29, 32.

[2] 1 Cor. xv. 45, viii. 6.

[3] Rom. ix. 5, Ὁ ὢν ἐπὶ πάντων θεός. The separation of these
words from the preceding, ὁ Χριστὸς τὸ κατὰ σάρκα, appears to
me forced and the less necessary as θεός in the sense of κύριος
occurs also 1 Cor. viii. 5 ; 2 Cor. iv. 4.

monotheism is strictly adhered to by Paul : God is
the absolute cause and end of all existence, including that of the Son, who has in God his head, is
conscious of being as the Father's possession bound
to serve Him, and, indeed, after the completion of
his work, will be subordinate to Him in such a way
that God alone will be all in all, none other inter-
vening.[1] Considered from this aspect, Christ is therefore as truly the archetypal image of man as he is,
on the other hand, the image of God ; it is his celestial image which we shall sometime bear, into likeness to which the elect will be fashioned, into which
they will be transformed.[2] This intermediate position
between God and man assigned to Christ is expressed
particularly plainly in the passage (1 Cor. xi. 3),
according to which Christ is the head of every man,
and God the head of Christ. As " the head of every
man," Christ is the creative archetype by which
and after which the earthly Adam was created; he
is therefore the celestial First Man, or ideal Man, in
whom mankind beholds its likeness to God repre-

---

[1] 1 Cor. iii. 23, xi. 3, xv. 28 ; Rom. vi. 10.

[2] 1 Cor. xv. 48, 49 ; Rom. viii. 29 ; 2 Cor. iv. 18 ; Phil. iii. 21.

sented and anticipated, but who does not enter into
the earthly phenomenal world until after the natural
man, and is therefore called "the last Adam, the
second Man from heaven."[1] It is the less allowable
to overlook this side of the Pauline Christology, as
it is of essential importance in its bearing on his
doctrine of atonement, as we shall soon see; nor
is it in any way inconsistent with the other side
of it—the holy spirituality and divine sonship of
Christ; in fact, according to Paul, the earthly
man ($\dot{a}\nu\acute{\eta}\rho$) is an image and ray of God, and we
are really all intended to become sons of God and
spiritual men.[2] Paul sees, therefore, that which
men are intended to *become* according to the Divine
purpose *realized*, in archetypal and primæval manner, in Christ as the celestial man; for which reason
he calls him also "the first-born amongst many
brethren." As such, he can also represent his
brethren before God, by entering into fellowship with
them, taking their guilt upon himself, and transfer-

---

[1] 1 Cor. xv. 45, 47.

[2] 1 Cor. xi. 7; Rom. viii. 29, 9, 14 sq.; Gal. iii. 26.

ring his righteousness to them. For this very purpose, Paul goes on to teach, God has sent his Son into terrestrial life, in a body of flesh similar to our own and by means of birth from a woman.[1] As Paul understood it, this was not an "incarnation" (*Menschwerdung*) in the strict doctrinal sense, inasmuch as the Son of God was really the celestial man and head of the human race before his appearance on the earth; he did not need therefore to take upon him a human nature, as orthodox theology teaches, but, according to Paul, he simply exchanged the form of his celestial existence, or his godlike body of light, for the earthly form of existence, or a body of flesh like that of men. This emptying and humiliation of himself to earthly poverty and servitude was an act of obedience to the will of God and of love to his human brethren.[2] According to Paul, therefore, the terrestrial Jesus is the appearance of the celestial Son of God and archetypal man Christ clothed in a body

---

[1] Rom. viii. 3 ; Gal. iv. 4.

[2] 2 Cor. viii. 9 ; Phil. ii. 5, 6.

of flesh, which we may express in modern forms of thought by saying, *he is the embodied Ideal of religious and divine humanity, of its filial relationship to God and of fraternal love between its own members.*

We might therefore regard it, according to our mode of thought, as most natural and probable that precisely this appearance of a holy human life was the object of the sending of Christ and the means of the salvation of the sinful world. However, frequently as the teaching of Paul is thus interpreted, particularly in recent theology, such was by no means his idea. If it had been, how could the earthly life of Jesus have been of such little importance to him, as we have seen was actually the case? On the contrary, that the *death* rather than the life of Jesus should be regarded by Paul as the divinely-ordained means of salvation, undoubtedly corresponds much more closely with the origin of his Christology. According to his view, Christ was sent in human flesh—and under the Law —simply in order to die for us the death of the curse of the Law, and thereby to liberate us for ever from the curse and the servitude of the Law in every form and to make us sons of God. It cannot be the business of a historical study to criticise this doctrine, but only to understand it in its origin; and the more fully we understand the motive forces of it in Paul's own thought, the sooner shall we be able to distinguish its lasting truth from its historical form. What were the motive forces of it in his mind?

In the first place, it is beyond doubt that it was from the principles of Pharisaic theology that Paul started. In that theology the legal Jewish conception of the religious relation prevailed absolutely.[1] Every sin, according to the Jewish school, is a transgression which, in so far as it has not been made good, or atoned for, by voluntary penance, demands rigorous punishment. According to the Pharisaic view, forgiveness without penance is as little possible with God as in the law of states. But the divine righteousness requires simply that the Law shall in some way have its justice vin-

---

[1] I refer for the proofs of this to the account, derived from the original sources, given in Weber's *System der Altsynagogalen Theologie* (Leipzig, 1880), §§ 67—72.

dicated, it being a matter of indifference on whom the punishment is executed or by whom the atonement in satisfaction of the guilt is presented. The innocent, therefore, may pay the atonement for the guilty, and thereby redeem the latter from the punishment. Thus in Jewish theology the undeserved suffering of the righteous especially is regarded as a substitutionary means of atonement, the guilt-removing virtue of which may be turned to the benefit, or reckoned for the justification, of the members of their families, or even of the whole nation of Israel. The less a man needs of atonement for his own sins, the more to the advantage of others is the surrender of his life as an atoning sacrifice; on that account the death of distinguished godly men possesses an atoning and redeeming virtue for the entire nation equal to that of the great day of atonement.

It is obvious how natural it must have been for Paul to make use of these prevailing views of the Pharisaic theology in explanation of the death on the cross of the Messiah Jesus. They received, however, under his hands an entirely new application, by which the stereotyped legal Jewish form became the receptacle of an ideal and ethical thought of the greatest significance. This was primarily and especially connected with Paul's peculiar view of the person of Christ. Inasmuch as Christ is not simply a righteous man after the Jewish ideal, not merely an ordinary earthly man, but the holy Son of God and Man from heaven, he has not to suffer at all for sin of his own; his death, therefore, as the voluntary taking upon himself of the curse of the Law, may be reckoned exclusively to the advantage of others. And to whose advantage will it be reckoned? To that of the Jews only? But Christ is not merely a son of Abraham; he is much rather the archetypal Man from heaven, the representative Head of *all* men, who in his life and death therefore legally represents the entire race, just as everywhere the head of a family or of a nation acts on behalf of either collectively. If the one, therefore, who is the Head of all died for all, his death is not simply that of an individual, but it denotes the death of all; the death of the one representative of all has legally before the Divine tribunal the same validity as if it had been the death of all, as if they had all collectively died in and with their Head.[1]   But in that case the curse of the Law has been atoned for on behalf of all; for when once death has been inflicted, the claim of the Law has been satisfied; it has nothing more to condemn and nothing more to demand; in fact, it rules over a man only as long as he lives; after he is dead it possesses no more right and no more power.   As, then, all have died in and with their representative Head, the legal claim of the Law has been satisfied and annulled for all; they are dead in view of both its curse and its demands; it has lost its power and validity for all; all are now entirely free from it, and may become the possession of a new Lord.   In this sense, therefore, Paul conceives the death of Christ as the divinely-ordained propitiation by which God "reconciled the world unto himself, no more imputing to them their sins:" in this sense he says, God "sent his Son, born of a woman and put under the Law, that he might redeem them that were under the

---

[1] 2 Cor. v. 15.

Law, that we might receive the adoption of sons;" Christ has "redeemed us from the curse of the Law, being made a curse for us," or God "made him to be sin for us, that we might become the righteousness of God in him;" He "set him forth as a propitiation in his blood by faith," and "in his flesh condemned sin;" he "died once to sin," and with his death we also were made dead as regards sin and the Law by means of his slain body.[1]   In all these passages the subject is an atonement instituted by God in the death of Christ, by which the Law received its due, while at the same time its claims were cancelled once for all and for all men; it is an objective divine act of propitiation on behalf of the whole world, since the whole world, that is mankind, was represented in the propitiatory death of its Head.   We see how the Pauline universalism and antinomianism have their roots in the centre of his theology, in his "word of the Cross."

However, this view of the objective aspects of

---

[1] 2 Cor. v. 19, 21; Gal. iv. 4, iii. 13; Rom. viii. 3, iii. 25, vi. 10, 11, vii. 4.

the matter, according to which the reconciliation of the world in the death of Christ was effected by a divine act, forms only one side of it, to which we must at once add the other, the subjective aspect of it, without which we should most disastrously misunderstand the Apostle's meaning. The objective reconciliation of the world effected in Christ's death can, after all, benefit actually in their own personal consciousness only those who know and acknowledge it, who know and feel themselves in their solidarity with Christ to be so much one with him as to be able to appropriate inwardly his death and celestial life, and inwardly live over again his life and death; those only, in a word, who truly *believe* on Christ. Thus the idea of " substitution " in Paul's view receives its complement and realization in the mysticism of his conception of faith. While Christ as the celestial Man objectively represents the whole race, that relation becomes a subjective reality of the religious consciousness only in the case of those who connect themselves with him in faith in such a way as to grow together with him into *one* spirit and *one* body, as to find in him their head, their soul, their life and self, and he in them his body, his members and his temple.[1] Thereby the idea of "one for all" receives the stricter meaning of "all in and with one:" thus regarded, the death of Christ is no longer merely the once occurring outward fact, which avails instead of the death of all by mere forensic substitution or imputation, but it becomes to a certain extent the actual ethical experience of the believers themselves, their common inward fellowship with Christ in his life and death. The Law possesses, therefore, no more claim of any kind upon these partakers with Christ in his life and death than upon Christ himself; its curse has been removed from them; their guilt has been cancelled; they have therefore been acquitted, justified before God, and are at peace with Him. And with this the servile spirit of fear gives place to the filial spirit of confidence, which plants in the heart the assurance of the love of God, and therewith creates grateful and obedient love to God and Christ in

---

[1] 1 Cor. vi. 17, 15, 19; Rom. vi. 5, 8, 9, 10; Gal. ii. 20; Phil. i. 21, iii. 9, 10.

return. When, in baptism, as the sacramental act of faith, the believer has "put on Christ," that is, has become personally one with him,[1] he has at the same time entered into a new relation to God: God beholds him no longer as the sinner he once was, but as the new man he now is in Christ, and so as sharing the righteousness of Christ; on the other hand, man no longer looks upon God as the angry Judge, but as the Father, who has guaranteed His love to all His sons in His first-born Son. Hence in the fact that one died for all, and all feel they have died and live with him, in truth, old things have passed away and all things have become new, a new creature, conscious of being in Christ reconciled to God and righteous before Him;[2] the ideal of a son of God has in the heart of the believer been transformed into the living reality of the conscious and felt relationship of a child to God. It is only when this is perceived that the Pauline doctrine of atonement is understood in its full meaning.

---

[1] Gal. iii. 27. [2] 2 Cor. v. 17, 21.

If from this position we now glance back to the starting-point of this doctrine, we at once perceive that we have reached, at the end of the way we have trodden, an entirely different conception of God from that from which we set out. *There* it was still the God of the Jewish *legal* consciousness, the righteous Judge, who does not mercifully forgive but who demands punishment or atonement, who will see the Law receive rigorously its due, even though he must execute its curse on His own Son. *Here*, on the contrary, it is the God of the Christian *filial* consciousness, as Jesus bore Him in his heart; the God of paternal love, who does not require from us atonement or satisfaction before He can forgive, who rather goes to meet the prodigal son, and from the fulness of His forgiving and beneficent love sets everything right. This double character of the Pauline conception of God is undoubtedly psychologically quite intelligible: it is the two souls which were always in conflict with each other in Paul's breast that are reflected in it: the servile spirit of the Law and the filial spirit of the Gospel, Pharisaic thought and Christian feeling, the theology of the Rabbi and the experience of the Apostle. Now, it is true that these two aspects do not occupy such a position of equality towards each other as to keep Paul in an attitude of fruitless wavering between the two standpoints; but the one of them is everywhere only the starting-point and the other the goal of his dialectics; the one supplies only the instruments and forms of his argumentation, the other the living and eternal religious subject-matter. Nevertheless, it cannot be denied that precisely in this peculiar oscillation and wavering between two different conceptions of God, which, treated logically, exclude and cancel each other, consists the difficulty in understanding Paul's theology, and is found the explanation of the striking fact that in all ages it has been its lot to be most differently interpreted and estimated, and that it has so rarely been faithfully reproduced. Neither can it be denied that the theory of the vicarious atonement of Christ and the imputed righteousness of faith may present to the thinker serious difficulties of a logical and ethical nature, inasmuch as it is only a theory and object of intellectual belief; but in practical religious life these difficulties disappear of themselves, because in living faith, in the devotion of the heart to the personal ideal of the Son of God, a man really becomes inwardly a new creature, and in this new state of life is conscious of being reconciled to God, is therefore really righteous, that is, stands in the right filial relation to God, and therein finds likewise the strength of love required for right moral conduct towards his fellow-men.

It was just this practically beneficial consequence of his doctrine of faith which Paul had special reason to prove, inasmuch as he was compelled to hear from even his earliest opponents the accusation that it produced morally injurious effects. " Shall we continue in sin, that grace may abound ?" he makes his Judaizing opponents ask.[1] And he says in reply, " God forbid !   We who died to sin, how shall we any longer live therein ?   Or know ye not that all we who were baptized into Christ were baptized into his death ?   We were buried with him,

---

[1] Rom. vi. 1.

therefore, through baptism into his death, that like as Christ was raised from the dead through the glory of the Father, so we also might walk in newness of life. For if we have become united with him through the likeness of his death, we shall be also by that of his resurrection." In this instance also Paul goes back again to his central idea of mystical fellowship with Christ, as he sees it established in the confession of faith in baptism; but this time he draws the inferences from it in a new direction. As members of the crucified and risen Christ, Christians have likewise died as regards their old man and have entered upon a new existence. Therewith they have been redeemed from the curse and compulsion of the Law and have become free children of God. But together with this change of religious relation to God, the foundation of a new divine life has been laid, and that in the two-fold sense that both the obligation and the power to lead another life have been supplied. Christians are bound to lead a new life by the motive of gratitude towards the Lord, to whose act of love and self-sacrifice they owe their new and happy state. For "he died for all, that they who live should live no longer unto themselves, but unto him who died for them and rose again."[1] Their newly granted life is not their own independent property, which they may employ after their own or another's pleasure, but it belongs of right to the Lord who has bought them at so dear a price for his own possession. As, therefore, Christ lives as the exalted Lord only unto God, so in like manner the life of those who belong to him must be an unbroken service of God. The love of God and Christ must fill their heart, God's Spirit lead them to all that is good; their body must be His temple; their members, weapons of righteousness; their eating and drinking and all they do must redound to the glory of God. That same faith in Christ which has delivered Christians from the killing Law of the letter, has likewise made them subject to the life-giving Law of the spirit of Christ. This new Law is no longer merely an outward letter, which could only command and judge, but it is the inward

---

[1] 2 Cor. v. 15.

impulse of love, of enthusiasm, of devotion and
reverence, which desires nothing else than to please
and become like him who is its life, its highest
good, its true self.   This new Law of Christ, therefore, brings with the obligation likewise the power
of meeting it, for it is happily no longer a frigid
command, which would impose compulsion on the
resolves of the heart; it is, on the contrary, the
most living impulse of the inmost heart itself:
"The love of Christ constraineth us.   Therefore I
live no longer, but Christ liveth in me.   Sin will
no more have dominion over us, for we are not
under the Law, but under grace."[1]

It is evident that Paul has herewith propounded
a new divine principle of greatest moment, a principle equally far removed from both Heathen license
and Jewish legalism.   In the reverent love of the
divine ideal of life which he beheld personified in
Christ, he found that inward freedom which was
raised as far above the Jewish servitude of ordinances as it was above the Heathen servitude of

---

[1] 2 Cor. v. 5, 14 ; Gal. ii. 20 ; Rom. vi. 14.

the flesh and worldly lust—that inward freedom which, unlike that of the Stoics, for instance, is not purchased by the deadening of the affections, by the hardening of the soul in the heartless coldness of "apathy," but which bears within itself the source of all life and happiness—love, which is the fulfilling of the Law. On that account this ethical principle was able to influence diseased and rent humanity in a very different way from Stoicism, animating and rejuvenating, healing and uniting it. Whilst Stoic cosmopolitanism only produced indifference towards the natural ties and limitations of society, Christian love, as Paul proclaimed it, encircled the disunited nations and countries with a uniting bond, made Jews and Greeks, slaves and free men, man and woman, one in Christ.[1] Thereby the Apostle planted that tree of humanity in human society under the branches of which we still dwell, and find shelter and protection for our highest possessions. This meritorious service is not essentially lessened by the

---

[1] Gal. iii. 28.

fact that the thorough carrying out of this great new principle in some particular departments of moral life remained in Paul's case defective in several respects. It is in fact, to our feeling, somewhat surprising that the Apostle of Christian freedom should pronounce slavery a matter of indifference, and advise the slave to remain in his condition even when he might become free.[1] Neither does it answer to our conception of the importance of the judicial institutions of the state, when the Apostle forbids the Christians of Corinth to seek justice before the secular tribunals.[2] It really shocks our feeling of the sacred dignity of the marriage state, when Paul suffers it only as a necessary evil for the prevention of unchastity, and in general describes the unmarried state as better and holier.[3] In this respect Protestantism has carried out Paul's principle, "All things are yours," more consistently than he himself did, by completely setting aside the historically conditioned limita-

---

[1] 1 Cor. vii. 21.   [2] 1 Cor. vi. 1 sq.

[3] 1 Cor. vii. 1 sq., 7, 32 sq., 38, 40.

tions with which the Apostle himself was still
hampered.

These limitations arose partly from the expectation of the speedy return of Christ to close that
period of the world, an expectation which Paul
shared with the first Christians universally, and
partly from the dualistic view of the relation of
sense and spirit which Paul held in common with
his age generally.   The latter was one of those
points in which Jewish and Greek thought in
that age met in practical agreement, although the
theoretical principles were on each side different.
For it is certainly true that the Pauline antithesis of flesh and spirit must not without modifi-
cation be identified with that of Plato and Philo;
the Pauline antithesis did not originate in Greek
philosophy, but directly in Jewish theology, and
indirectly in the Old Testament.   The latter understood by "flesh" the earthly creature of sense, particularly mankind in its antithesis to God, whose
nature is supersensible and supermundane spirit,
the creative and holy energy of life.   And with the
idea of natural weakness and impurity, which belong

to the sense nature of flesh, was early connected, as, for instance, in the Book of Job,[1] the ethical idea of weakness and impurity, in virtue of which the flesh is made subject to both sin and death. This theory was afterwards combined by Rabbinic theology in a peculiar way with the doctrine of the fall of Adam. In consequence of that first sin, it was taught in the Synagogue, not death alone, but sin, prevailed amongst men; for the tendencies to evil, the possibility of which had existed from the beginning in the human body, thereupon attained a new and almost irresistible supremacy over the tendencies of the soul to good, and ruled human action with despotic power.[2] When, notwithstanding, Jewish theology imposed on man the duty of attaining to perfect righteousness by his own effort, it was in evident contradiction with the above psychological premises, a contradiction, moreover, similarly met with in the

---

[1] Job. iv. 17 sq., xiv. 4, xv. 14 sq. ; comp. also Gen. vi. 3; Ps. ciii. 14.

[2] Comp. Weber, *System der Altsynagogalen Theologie*, §§ 47 —50.

ethics of Stoicism of that period. Nor on this point of doctrine has Paul put forward anything like an entirely new theory, but only with greater rigour drawn out the Pharisaic theory into its consequences. Sin and death he conceives[1] as entering the world through Adam, and thenceforth ruling with royal despotism all men, who are, as children of Adam, sold by their fleshly nature to that sovereign power. For in the body, the earthly and sense part of the natural man, evil desire has set up its seat, or, as it were, its citadel, whence, by means of the tendencies and impulses of the flesh in the members, it makes the will its servant, so that it brings forth all kinds of sin, not merely sins of a sensual but also of a spiritual nature, such as idolatry and selfish wickedness. It is true, the inward man, by virtue of the good impulses of his reason, can condemn the dominance of sin in his members, but he is unable actually to subdue it, because he is so sold under sin as to feel it as a

---

[1] Rom. v. 12—21, vii. 5, 13—25, viii. 7, 13 ; Gal. v. 17 sq. ; 1 Cor. xv. 21, 47—50.

"law," that is, as a constant despotic power which holds his better self in captivity. And against that "law," even the revealed Law of God, holy and good as it is, avails nothing, because it is weakened by sin in the flesh; in fact, it is, on the contrary, such as by its prohibition to provoke sin to fuller development. With this Paul established by the anthropological method the conviction (of which he had, moreover, become assured by dogmatical inferences from the atoning death of Christ), that by the works of the Law no flesh could become righteous. Why had previously all his eager endeavour after righteousness been in vain? Now he could answer that question, since he also knew the answer to another painful one, "O wretched man that I am, who will deliver me from the body of this death?" namely, "The law of the spirit of life in Christ hath made me free from the law of sin and of death!"

Just as Paul, when looking back upon his former condition from the new one of conscious salvation, formed such a profound conception of the hopeless ruin of the natural man as ruled by the sin in his flesh, that he spoke of a "law of sin," so with like profundity he recognized the new life in Christ as a "law of the spirit." With that conception, again, he gave to a traditionary idea a new turn of the greatest significance and rich in results. In the First Church it was already an established supposition that the holy spirit was received by faith and baptism into the Messiah, a supposition which was based on Old Testament promises of the outpouring of the spirit at the time of salvation.[1] But as the holy spirit in the Old Testament was not conceived as the constant inward principle of life in the people of God, but as a supernatural divine power, which descended temporarily upon individuals and produced extraordinary effects for definite purposes, so likewise in the First Church it was conceived as the supernatural divine power which called forth extraordinary states and efforts of a remarkable kind. Thus the ecstatic condition of speaking with tongues, the apocalyptic gift of prophecy, the individual gift of the "word of wisdom,"

---

[1] Acts ii. 33, 38, x. 44, 45 ; comp. Joel iii. 1 ; Ezek. xxxvi. 27.

the special power of faith for miraculous cures and
similar extraordinary *charismata*, were looked upon
as the works and signs of the Messianic spirit, those
speaking with tongues in Corinth, for instance, being
regarded as "spiritual men" pre-eminently.[1] Paul,
it is true, shared that view; he did not, however,
rest satisfied with it, but extended and deepened
the significance of the spirit. Feeling himself by
his faith in the Lord, who is the spirit, made into
one spirit with him, he saw in the holy spirit the
indwelling and constant principle, or "law," of
his new life, and a principle which does not manifest itself merely in certain extraordinary impulses
and miraculous powers, but as the creative energy
of a "new creature," in the renewing of the heart,
in the sanctification of the entire life, in the generation of every Christian virtue, in a growing likeness to the image of Christ. The spirit of Christ
manifests itself not merely in the mystical con-
vulsions of an obscure and speechless emotional
excitement, but in the distinct and calm feeling

---

[1] 1 Cor. xii. 14.

of the peace and joy of a child of God conscious of being reconciled with its Father;[1] not merely in apocalyptic visions of miraculous things in the future, but in a clear and reasonable knowledge of those things which have been given us by God, and in a wide view of the wonderful ways and judgments of God in the course of the world's history;[2] not merely in theurgic powers and miraculous operations of an abrupt character, but in the constant moral power of love, which is the greatest of miracles.[3] Herewith Paul inaugurated that decisive change of view by which Christianity made the transition from the miraculous world of ecstatic feeling and apocalyptic phantasy, into the true spiritual world of religious and moral personal life, and by which it could become the regenerating leaven of the history of mankind. Not as if he had on that account set aside or disregarded the

---

[1] Rom. v. 5, viii. 15, 38, xv. 13; Gal. iv. 6, v. 22.

[2] 1 Cor. ii. 7—16, xii. 8.

[3] 1 Cor. xii. 31—xiii. 13; Gal. v. 6, 13, 22; Rom. xiii. 10, xiv. 17 sq.

apocalyptic future hopes of the First Church; no, the expectation of the speedy return of Christ, of the resurrection of the dead, of the last judgment and end of the world, was as certain and as important to him as to any one of the earliest Christians; but knowing that he already possessed, as a present inner reality and operative power,[1] the Christian spirit of the new life of the kingdom of God, which others looked for only in the miraculous catastrophes of the future, he bridged over the chasm dividing the next world from this, transforming the transcendental Messianic kingdom of Jewish and primitive Christian hope into the moral kingdom of God of the Christian Church, with its "life in the spirit" and its faith and love. With this, however, Paul had only given a new theological turn to the thought which Jesus had given expression to in his popular parables of the Mustard-seed and the Leaven, thereby preserving that mustard-seed from the danger of being choked by the luxuriantly rampant branches of apocalyptic phantasy.

---

[1] Rom. vi. 4, vii. 6, viii. 9, 10, xiv. 17; 2 Cor. iv. 7 sq., v. 17, vi. 2, 10; Gal. v. 6, 25.

That a religious idea of such mystical and speculative profundity as the Pauline doctrine of the
holy spirit, however, might take root in the consciousness of the Church, it necessarily required a
somewhat massive outward shell, which might protect and preserve the noble fruit within, while
at the same time it concealed and made it un-
recognizable to the superficial eye. A shell of
this kind was supplied not only in dogmatic Christology as founded by Paul and further carried out
by the theology of the Church, but also in the
mystical view of the sacraments. In this respect
also Paul put an original construction on traditional usages, bringing them into the closest relation
with the central idea of his theology. *Baptism*,
which in the First Church had been only a public
act of repentance and profession, became in Paul's
theology[1] a mystical act of implantation in the
fellowship of Christ's life and death by means of a
sacramental imitation and appropriation of the act
of redemption effected originally and typically in

---

[1] Rom. vi. 3 sq.; Gal. iii. 27.

Christ; for in immersion beneath the water, Christ's death and burial, and in emersion from the water, his resurrection, are imitated in dramatic symbolism. Thus baptism became the sacrament of regeneration through the spirit, by which the old life of the sinful flesh was done away with, and a new creature, a holy spiritual life devoted to God, was born and incorporated as a living member with the body of Christ. The meals of love of the First Church likewise received first from Paul[1] the significance of strictly sacramental acts of worship. When the Church solemnizes the *Lord's Supper*, the partaking of the consecrated cup and bread is not simply a symbolical act in remembrance of the shed blood and the broken body of Christ, but it is also the means of effecting a mystical union with the crucified Head of the Church; for they who partake of those symbols of his death thereby inwardly appropriate the death of Christ himself, entering thus into the closest covenant with him and one another for life and death. But as the counterpart of this mys-

---

[1] 1 Cor. x. 16 sq., xi. 23—30.

terious union with Christ, realized in a devout observance of the rite, must be placed the punitive effect
of an undevout observance of it, which Paul is disposed to discover in the cases of sickness and death
occurring in the Church. The affinity of ideas of
this kind with certain features of Heathen sacrifices
and mysteries, was referred to even by Paul himself,
and was variously dwelt upon by the Church Fathers;
neither can it be denied that the subsequent grosser
conceptions of the doctrine of the sacraments held
by the Church were naturally connected with this
Pauline theory of the sacraments of Baptism and
the Eucharist. Nevertheless, it is only those who
can find it conceivable that the Church could have
been satisfied with a cultus with no mysteries who
will on that account raise a complaint against
Paul. That he discovered, by reference to the
central fact of salvation in the death of Christ,
the means of satisfying the need, founded in human
nature, of a mystical cultus, we are convinced is
one of those marvellous inspirations of genius on
which history itself has set its seal, and which
we, therefore, ought not to criticise with cold

rationalism, but to honour with thankful and reverent piety.

In possession of that spirit which searches even the depths of Deity, Paul finally obtained new and profound insight into the counsels and ways of the Divine government of the world. Starting from the anticipations of the Prophets, but giving them a deeper meaning in the light of the Christian idea of salvation, he sketched a new philosophy of religious history, which served as a magnificent historical setting and proof for his theological ideas. He was led to it by the necessity of justifying his teaching and labours to the Jewish and Jewish-Christian mind, which had taken serious offence especially at two points: one of which concerned the Pauline view of the Mosaic Law; the other, the actual result of his mission to the Heathen, in consequence of which the Heathen Christians grew every day more important than the Jewish Christians. When Paul taught that Christ was the end of the Law and was sent to redeem us from the Law,[1] it appeared to the Jew that the character of

---

[1] Rom. x. 4 ; Gal. iv. 5.

revelation belonging to the Law was thereby denied; for, he asked, how could a Law given by God be transient? And when, by the conversion of large numbers of the Heathen, the Jewish portion of the Messianic Church was more and more outstripped and reduced to a minority, the promises of the Prophets, which were given, surely, in the first instance and principally to the children of Abraham, seemed to the Jew to lose their validity. The Law and the Prophets, the entire Oracles of God, seemed therefore to be rendered doubtful by Paul. How could that accord with the will of God, whose word is undoubtedly incapable of change or failure? And how could it accord with the intention of the Messiah Jesus, who had said, surely, that he had not come to destroy, but to fulfil the Law and the Prophets? Paul was the more urgently led to remove such natural scruples, as the divine revelation of the Law and the Prophets was, beyond doubt, to himself likewise an established certainty. The task before him was, therefore, to reconcile this conviction, held no less firmly by himself than by his opponents, with his doctrine of the end of the Mosaic Law and of the call of the Heathen into the Messianic kingdom. The task was, in fact, not easy, and Paul brought to its accomplishment all the acuteness of his Rabbinical dialectics and all the profundity of his Christian gnosis.

From our modern point of view, we might perhaps suppose that the simplest means of reconciling the transient nature of the Mosaic Law with its revealed origin, would have been to distinguish between its ethical and ceremonial constituents. The Pauline doctrine of the Law has often been understood as if his contention had been directed against the ceremonial Law only, which he is supposed to have distinguished from the moral precepts, as the perishable from the eternal element. But this distinction is opposed to the proper sense of Paul's theory of the Law. He shared, on the contrary, with the Jews generally the supposition that the Law was an indivisible whole, and in all its parts an immediate divine revelation; a criticism of the matter of the Law, a distinction between its lasting and transient elements, was, therefore, quite out of the question in Paul's case. In order to reach

his object, he was obliged accordingly to adopt
another course—the historico-teleological method.
With a boldness of paradox such as is possible only
to a religious genius, Paul undertook to prove, from
the history of divine revelation itself, the transient
nature of the revealed Law. The point at which he
applied the lever of his method of proof was the relation of the Law to the promises. This very relation
had beyond doubt already often occupied the attention of the Pharisee Paul; indeed, the profoundest
antinomy, the most trying enigma of the Pharisaic
theology, was involved precisely in the fact, that
the immediate fulfilment of the promises by God
was expected, while at the same time it was
believed to be conditioned by the complete fulfilment on man's part of the Law, a fulfilment which
had always been and still remained incomplete.
The solution of this enigma, which was impossible
from the Jewish point of view, dawned upon Paul
at the cross of Christ: with the certainty that God
on His part offers us, as a gift of grace through
Christ, the righteousness we cannot possibly fulfil,
the conclusion was of itself suggested to him, that

in that case the Law could not from the first have been given with the purpose of making the Divine fulfilment of the promises dependent on its fulfilment by man. But then the question arose, For what end can the Law have been given by God, if it is not meant to be the condition of the attainment of salvation? To this Paul replies with the bold paradox, The Law came in between the promise and the fulfilment, not in order to bring about righteousness, which it can never do, and by which it would really annul the grace of the promise, but, on the contrary, in order to occasion transgression, to provoke the sinful desires of the flesh to activity, to bring to painful consciousness the guilt of sin—in a word, to hold mankind captive under the ban of the wretchedness of sin, until the longed-for salvation through the grace of God in Christ should come.[1] The Law is, according to this, given by God, it is true, and forms an essential member in the economy of the Divine plan of salvation, the object of which is

---

[1] Gal. iii. 19—24 ; Rom. v. 20, 21, iv. 15, iii. 20, vii. 5, 7—13, xi. 32.

the formation of a holy people of God; but the
Law does not promote this object as a direct and
positive means of righteousness, as the Jew supposed, but only indirectly and negatively, inasmuch
as it is in the first instance really a means of
unrighteousness, of the increase of sin, of producing
the consciousness of guilt and helplessness and the
sense of the need of redemption.   Thus the Law
had from the first only the importance of a perishable instrument, the destiny of which was to pass
away when its object had been attained; it was
intended as a schoolmaster to keep mankind, while
in its minority, in subjection until the time when
with faith in the Son of God the freedom of the
full-aged sons of God should appear.

From this point of view the history of mankind
divides itself in the Apostle's mind into three ages,
which correspond, again, to the three principles
of Promise, Law and Fulfilment, or to the three
typical names of Abraham, Moses and Christ.   The
first age is that of the Patriarchs, when faith in the
promise still ruled without law;[1] that is the age of

---

[1] Gal. iii. 16—18; Rom. iv. 5, 13.

the childhood of the race, the happy period of inno-
cence, when sin was still unknown, because nothing
was then known of the command, "Thou shalt not
indulge desire."[1] Then comes the Law of Moses, as
the schoolmaster who keeps the youth under the
compulsion of his commands and prohibitions, and
thereby provokes his will to resistance, calls into
existence his desire to transgress, and holds the
transgressor captive under the torture of the sense
of guilt;[2] that is the age of the covenant of the
Law, the transient nature of which the Apostle sees
symbolized in the vanishing of the glorious light on
the countenance of Moses.[3] At last, at the time
appointed by God, the fulfilment of the promise,
and therewith the end of the covenant of Law,
appeared; for by faith in the Son of God we have
become sons of God, who are no longer under the
pædagogue: for the servile spirit of fear has been
substituted the filial spirit of confidence, which finds
its early prototype in the faith of Abraham. But the

---

[1] Rom. vii. 7.

[2] Gal. iii. 23 sq., iv. 1 sq.; Rom. vii. 8 sq.

[3] 2 Cor. iii. 13 sq.

divine covenant of promise made with the Fathers
has now been fulfilled in a higher form; for the
contradiction between desire and duty, which in
their time was only prospective, has now been overcome and reconciled in that spirit of sonship which
is at the same time a spirit of freedom and love.
On this account the new covenant of the spirit is an
eternal covenant, the glory of which remains for ever.

Thus the enigma and the stumbling-block to the
Jewish mind involved in the idea of the Law being
a divine revelation and yet of transient validity,
were in the Apostle's case removed by the supposition of a divine education of the human race.
And the same point of view of a divine teleology
conducts him likewise to the solution of the other
enigma, namely, of the possibility of the nation to
which the promises were given being outstripped in
the Messianic kingdom by the Gentiles. First of
all,[1] it is true, Paul points the Jews, who see in
this order of things a violation of the prerogatives
promised to them, to the unconditionality of the

---

[1] Rom. ix. 6—29.

Divine will, to contend with which is altogether unbecoming in the creature. Just as God in the times of the Patriarchs, by the free choice of His grace, had mercy on the one and rejected the other, so now again it is His free grace which permits the Gentiles to experience His compassion. And Israel's hardening, he goes on to show,[1] is nothing surprising, but simply proves once more that it continues to be the same stiff-necked and rebellious people of which the Prophets had from the beginning to complain, so that its remaining behind the Gentiles is as much its own fault as God's appointment. Nevertheless, God had not therein Israel's definitive loss in view; His word of promise has not for ever lost its validity. It is only temporarily that He has caused the Jews to fall behind, with the design that their holding aloof might make possible the approach of the Gentiles, and their loss promote the Gentiles' gain. But when once this object has been attained, when once the fulness of the Heathen has entered into the kingdom of God, then will come Israel's

---

[1] Rom. ix. 30—x. 21.

turn to be received; the precedence of the Heathen will provoke those who are now rebellious to jealous imitation, and thus the gracious purposes of God will finally be accomplished in the case of all.[1] All the wonderful ways and leadings of the world's history, not excepting even the sin and error of men, must at last serve as means of promoting the plan of salvation projected by Divine love and wisdom. Thus all the contradictions of time are harmoniously reconciled in the knowledge of that God from whom and through whom and to whom are all things!

---

[1] Rom. xi.

THE CONFLICT OF THE APOSTLE TO THE GENTILES WITH JEWISH CHRISTIANS.

THE CONFLICT OF THE APOSTLE TO THE GENTILES WITH JEWISH CHRISTIANS.

A GLANCE in our last Lecture at the chief points of Paul's teaching has fully confirmed the Apostle's claim with regard to his gospel, namely, that it was an original creation of an inward revelation of the spirit of Christ, independent of the tradition of the First Church, and differing from it in essential points. In such circumstances, instead of being astonished that it came at last to animated conflicts between Paul and the Jewish Christians, we must rather be surprised that those conflicts did not break out much earlier. During the fourteen years of his first missionary labours in the regions of Syria and Cilicia, such unbroken harmony existed between himself and the churches of Judea, that,

according to his own statement, they praised God
for the fruits of his mission.[1] It is possible that
Paul himself had not then realized the full consequences involved in his principles with regard
to Christian freedom from the Law; it is likewise
possible that in Judea no accurate information was
possessed regarding the state of things in churches
at a considerable distance, or that, in delight at the
general results, the mixture of the Gentile Christian
elements and the free intercourse of the Jewish
with the Gentile believers were overlooked.   But
when, with the further extension of the mission of
Paul into Heathen territory, increasing numbers of
Heathen churches were formed, and at the same
time in the church of the Syrian capital, Antioch,
the Gentile element grew so largely in numbers and
influence that the action of the whole community
there took a constantly freer form, this development
of things began to excite attention in Jerusalem,
and the simple unrestrained delight at Paul's success gave place to mistrustful anxiety as to the

---

[1] Gal. i. 21.

incalculable consequences of such proceedings. The most zealous considered it wrong to continue inactive spectators of the Apostle's line of action, and went themselves to Antioch to observe and to oppose on the spot the freer customs that had sprung up. The agitation set on foot by these "false brethren brought in unawares," as Paul describes them,[1] threw the mixed community at Antioch into no little commotion, especially as these people naturally appealed to the authority of the parent church.

We may imagine in what a painful situation the Apostle Paul consequently found himself. If the party zealous for the Law should be successful with their demand that the believing Gentiles must by circumcision submit to the Jewish Law, and if it should be confirmed that in this demand they really had the parent church, together with the Apostles, on their side, the mission to the Gentiles was at an end, the life-work of the Apostle to the Heathen was hopeless. For if he had submitted to their requirement of the Law, there was

---

[1] Gal. ii. 4 ; comp. Acts xv. 1.

no more room to hope for any great success in
his mission to the Heathen, the Jewish Law would
have become an invincible hindrance to the conversion of the Heathen to Christ.   If Paul had, on
the other hand, simply ignored the demands of the
Judaizers, without coming to any understanding
with the earlier Apostles and obtaining their sanction for his Gentile mission, with its freedom from
the Law, he would have severed the connection of
his Heathen churches with the parent church, and
the Gentile Church, thus isolated from the very
first and degraded to a sect, would hardly have
been able long to maintain its existence.   The continuance or the destruction of his life-work depended
therefore now, to Paul's mind, on whether he succeeded in obtaining from the parent church and
its leaders the acknowledgment of their Christian
fellowship for his Gentile Christians as such.   In
this critical moment, as Paul himself relates, it was
the inward spiritual voice of a "revelation" which
matured in his mind the resolution to overcome
the crisis by the most direct, though, it must be
allowed, the most hazardous course—by a personal

discussion of the matter with the parent church, and especially with its principal leaders. Paul naturally communicated his plan, which so closely concerned it, to the church at Antioch; and the church must then have sanctioned his proposal and adopted it as the resolution of the body, and accordingly deputed the Apostle himself, together with Barnabas, as its official and trusted delegates to Jerusalem. This public sanction of the journey to Jerusalem, as it is reported in the Acts of the Apostles, is so far from excluding the origin of it as related by Paul himself, that, on the contrary, the two accounts admirably complete each other. The same may be said substantially of the accounts of the course of the subsequent transactions at Jerusalem; the agreement as to the chief points is in any case greater than the discrepancies in the details, and these discrepancies can be for the most part explained simply by the difference of the standpoint of the relaters.

When Paul made his report as to his missionary labours and their results in the Heathen world to a meeting of the church at Jerusalem (for the account in the Epistle to the Galatians likewise compels us to suppose such a meeting), that party of zealots, to whom the "false brethren" and agitators who had crept into Antioch belonged, put forward the demand, that the converted Gentiles must be made Jews by circumcision, and that that regulation must at once be put in force by the circumcision of Titus, the Gentile companion of Paul on his journey. Paul does not tell us directly what was the reply of the meeting of the church to this requirement, yet he supplies the data for probable conjecture. In the first place, we must observe that Paul mentions, as the real occasion of the animated contention as to the circumcision of Titus, the "false brethren" that had crept in, obviously distinguishing them, therefore, as the more decided zealots, from the rest of the church. We must neither overlook nor over-estimate the importance of this distinction. Nowhere do we meet with any such statement as that the whole church was from the first quite on the side of Paul, and that the zealots of the Law formed merely an insignificant fraction. On the contrary, we cannot shut our eyes to the fact, that, assuming the truth of this traditional supposition, it would be hard to comprehend how such animated contentions could arise as are undeniably recorded in both accounts alike (Gal. ii. and Acts xv.). The most probable conjecture is, therefore, that when the question was proposed to the church at Jerusalem thus definitely, whether in future there should be a Christianity without the Mosaic Law, its members at first took up no definite position with regard to it, but wavered indecisively between opposing opinions and considerations. To their strictly conservative Jewish mind it was undoubtedly a very unfamiliar idea, that they should in the future acknowledge, as brothers in faith in the Messiah, Heathen without the Law, who had hitherto always been looked upon by them as unclean and sinners. It was to be feared, too, that by such fraternization the reputation of the young Christian Church would be seriously compromised in the eyes of the Jewish people, and its reputation for righteousness greatly shaken, which naturally would not be favourable to the success of the mission to Israel itself. Moreover, the question might well arise, whether it was possible that the Messiah Jesus, who notoriously sought not to destroy but to fulfil the Law, would acknowledge those who did not adopt the Law as fellow-citizens of the kingdom, when he should come in the immediate future to set it up. Under the influence of doubts of this kind, the feeling of the church undoubtedly inclined at first to favour the demands of the party zealous for the Law. On the other hand, however, it was after all unable to escape from the force of the impression which the reports of Paul and Barnabas as to their past successes amongst the Gentiles had produced. Was not the church obliged to discern therein practical proof that the Heathen mission was an undertaking well-pleasing to God? And had not even the Prophets foretold the coming in of the Gentiles in the days of the consummation? Were not also certain utterances of Jesus current which represented the faith of the Heathen as an example fitted to shame the unbelieving Jews? With all its Jewish conservatism, the parent church cannot have been wholly impervious to such considerations. Nevertheless, the solitary Paul, the daring innovator, evidently held a trying position against the multitude of those who had the stubborn power of custom and the scrupulous loyalty of the Jewish conscience on their side.

It was in reality therefore an extremely critical moment, on the issue of which hung nothing less than the future of Christianity; the battle of opinions inclined first to the one side and then to the other, when the chief Apostles threw their vote into the scale in favour of free Heathen Christianity. Beyond doubt, the Acts of the Apostles has reported correctly when it describes Peter as taking the initiative in that direction: although the speech which this book puts into his mouth betrays traces of the later date of its editor, we cannot doubt that it was the decisiveness of Peter's temperament, and still more his unreserved love of the Lord Jesus, which caused him to put aside all other considerations and extend to the Apostle of the Gentiles the right-hand of fellowship. This act of noble, self-denying magnanimity saved the future of Christianity in a critical moment; and for that reason

the Church justly holds the memory of Peter in
high honour. James, the brother of the Lord, and
the Apostle John likewise, followed the example
of Peter and confirmed the bond of brotherhood;
but they (at all events James) did not do this as
unreservedly as Peter. For undoubtedly the Acts
of the Apostles is justified in making the narrower
and more strictly Jewish spirit of James account-
able for the conditions by which the fraternal alliance
was restricted; he, moreover, not having belonged,
like Peter, to the number of the Apostles of Jesus,
was not so much influenced by his free spirit. As
regards the conditions of the agreement, the two
accounts differ. According to Paul, they were
simply, first, that the sphere of his Heathen mission and that of the Jewish mission of the other
Apostles should in future also remain separate;
secondly, that Paul should remember the poor of
the churches of Judea, that is, should collect charitable gifts for them amongst the Heathen.[1] The
Acts of the Apostles is silent as to these two

---

[1] Gal. ii. 9, 10.

points, and states instead that in a formal resolution
of the Church the obligation was imposed on the
Heathen Christians of abstaining from meat offered
to idols, from fornication, from blood, and from things
strangled.[1]

This difference between the two accounts has
been made the subject of much debate, to enter
upon which in detail would on this occasion occupy
too much of our time: I must confine myself to the
following observations. As Paul does not mention
in any way these four obligations imposed on the
Gentiles, but, on the contrary, asserts that nothing
was required of him by those of reputation, save
that he should remember the poor, and as subsequently, in speaking of the eating of flesh offered
to idols, he does not even distantly allude to a resolution of the Apostles bearing upon it, the doubt
as to the historical character of the resolution is
probably well founded. However, it does not by
any means follow from this supposition that the
author of the Acts arbitrarily invented his narrative,

---

[1] Acts xv. 20, 28, 29.

and with a definite dogmatic purpose. We must, on the contrary, keep in view the fact that the four conditions of James correspond substantially to the obligations which were at that time generally imposed on the Proselytes of the Gate. When, therefore, we remember that the first Heathen Christians were for the most part from the Proselytes of the Gate, the conjecture naturally presents itself that those Proselytes will as Christians have continued their former manner of life, and that accordingly the observance of the Proselytes' commands must from the first have become the standing practice of the Gentile Christians in certain churches. We need not think it at all surprising or objectionable that a practice of this kind, which had of itself grown up, should in the tradition of the Church be referred to a special apostolic regulation, and that it should be placed *bonâ fide* by the author of the Acts in direct connection with the Apostolic Council. However, the further possibility appears to me not altogether out of the question, namely, that after an agreement had been come to in Jerusalem as to the chief matter, the other points were subsequently discussed, in some such way as this—that on the Jewish side the expectation was expressed, and on the other side the promise given, that the Gentile Christians should continue as before to observe the Proselytes' commands, in order that no offence might be given to the consciences of the Jews in the Diaspora. Such a subsidiary agreement, which followed almost as a matter of course, Paul might very well all along ignore, while the author of the Acts was acquainted with it through the traditions of the church at Antioch, and looked upon it as the principal matter of the contract, inasmuch as he possessed no particular information about the more personal arrangements come to between Paul and the First Church. In this way a reconciliation of the two accounts may be conceived as at all events not impossible. Moreover, I am of opinion that this question has not in reality the great importance which is often attached to it; for whether the removal of this special difference is thought to be possible or not, appears to me to be of quite secondary moment in view of the unquestionable fact, that with regard to the real meaning and object of the Apostles' agreement the accounts of

Paul and of the Acts conduct to essentially unanimous results.

I find those results in the following three points:
1. The freedom of Gentile Christians from the Jewish Law was conceded. 2. The continuance of the validity of that Law in the case of Jewish Christians was pre-supposed as a matter of course. 3. The restrictive conditions of the agreement were meant in the minds of the Jewish Christians to protect the legal position of Jewish Christianity from all the dangers which threatened it from contact with Heathen Christians, and to assimilate the relation of Heathen to Jewish Christians to that of Proselytes to Jews, or of partial members to full members of the kingdom of God. With the first and most important point Paul had gained the essential object of his journey : the question as to the right of Heathen Christianity to exist without an acknowledgment of the Law had been decided in the affirmative by the parent church and its chief men. With that decision faith in the Messiah Jesus was acknowledged as constituting a new common religious life, superior to the distinction of Jew and Gentile ;

Christianity was accordingly placed as a new religion upon a footing of its own, and definitely distinguished from Judaism, with which it had hitherto been amalgamated as a smaller society or sect. This was at all events an attainment of great moment which could never be again wholly lost; the foundation for the edifice of the universal Christian Church had then been laid, the universalistic Christian faith of Paul, in conjunction with the practical large-heartedness of Peter, had victoriously held the field and overcome Jewish particularism. Yet it was undoubtedly a long way from this point to the complete union of both parties in one Church. Though they were associated by the ideal bond of their common faith in Christ, they continued to be divided as before by the remaining wall of separation created by the Mosaic Law. For the conclusion which appears to us so obvious—that if the Law is not binding on Gentile Christians it must cease to be binding on Jewish Christians—was quite foreign to the mind of the parent church, including its chief men, not only at the Apostolic Council, but afterwards. This is one of the most indubitable and also,

I

for the history of early Christianity, one of the most important facts. It is only by means of it that the division in the spheres of missionary labour between Paul and Peter can be properly understood: that division was the natural consequence of the obligation still resting on the first Apostles to observe the Jewish Law, which rendered missionary labours amongst the Gentiles impossible in their case, on account of the unavoidable observance of the laws regarding purification; that division was also meant to serve as a guarantee for the protection of the legal position of the Jewish Christians against the seductive influence of the anti-legal procedure of the Pauline mission. It is only by means of this fact that the vacillating conduct of Peter at Antioch, the action and the success of the emissaries of James in that city, and the entire subsequent contest of the Judaists against Paul generally, can be understood. Finally, we have direct evidence in the words of James himself, when, Acts xxi. 21, he expressly speaks of the Jewish Christians as men "zealous for the Law," and represents the charge made against Paul, of seducing the Jews to renounce the Law of Moses, as an incredible aspersion. All these facts point concordantly to the conclusion, that in the First Church the Pauline conviction,—that faith in Christ was in principle irreconcilable with the religion of the Law, and that Christ was therefore the end of the Law for *all* Christians, Jews as well as Gentiles,—was after the Apostolic Council still as far as ever from having been reached. The concession which was made in the Council to the Heathen Christians was, therefore, not the result of a clear dogmatic perception of the unimportance of the Jewish Law for the Christian Church, but it had only been forced from the Jewish conscience by the overawing impression produced by Paul and the actual results of his work, in which it was impossible not to see a divine vindication of the rights of the Heathen Christians. But the First Church had not at the Council any idea that further inferences in the sense of the Pauline freedom from the Law must or might be drawn from that concession. And we regard this shortsightedness on its part as so far fortunate, as without it the acknowledgment of Heathen Christianity, with its freedom from the Law, would hardly have been ever brought about.

But it was just in this want of clearness and consistency that the weakness of the Apostolic agreement lay. It was a treaty of peace in which were hidden the germs of fresh dissensions. It aimed at effecting an external co-existence, side by side, of a Gentile Christianity independent of the Law and a Jewish Christianity loyal to the Law; but how could this division be carried out in mixed churches like that at Antioch? Under it, how could any intercourse between the two sections of a church, a united religious service, a common solemnization of the Lord's Supper, or generally any united church life, exist? If, therefore, the Christian consciousness of fraternal union nevertheless imperatively demanded such a church life, one of the two divisions would be obliged of necessity to accommodate itself to the other, and accordingly either the Heathen brethren would be compelled to live under the Law or the Jewish brethren to live without it. But then freedom from the Law had only just been accorded to the Heathen;

what was therefore more natural than that the Jewish Christians of Antioch should now, in the interests of the harmony of the church, participate more largely in the freedom of their Gentile brethren? The church at Antioch was thus on the way to successfully realize, under the eyes of its leaders, Paul and Barnabas, Christian freedom to an extent far outstripping the intention of the Apostolic agreement.

But how was this course which things were taking regarded in Jerusalem? At this point we are again met by the characteristic difference between Peter and James. The former did not hesitate to pay a visit to the liberal-minded church at Antioch, and with the inoffensive large-heartedness of his sanguine temperament to conform to its liberal practices. It was otherwise with James: he beheld in the freedom prevalent in Antioch a flagrant violation of the conditions of the agreement come to at Jerusalem, a disavowal of things sacred to the Jewish conscience, a lowering of the Righteous to the level of Heathen Sinners, a profanation of faith in the Messiah. And probably the majority in Jerusalem were of his way of thinking. Consequently a few started from that capital with a view of checking those free proceedings in Antioch, and particularly of whetting the edge of Peter's Jewish conscience. Their arrival produced a paralyzing effect on the more liberal and advanced spirit of the Antiochians; opposition to them was not ventured upon, their stricter principles were submitted to in timid embarrassment. Peter first of all withdrew from the Gentile Christians, with whom he had previously kept up an inoffensive fellowship at their tables; his example was soon followed by the other Jewish Christians, Barnabas even suffering himself to be carried away by the reactionary wave; indeed, the new scrupulous spirit had such an infectious influence that Heathen Christians felt themselves under a certain moral pressure, and appeared inclined to submit to the Jewish customs. Thereupon Paul could restrain himself no longer: with all the keen severity characteristic of him when questions of religious principle were at stake, he opposed Peter, and charged him plainly with dissembling, because he was not only himself renounc-

ing, but causing others to renounce, the freer principles which had only just before been in practice
acknowledged as valid.[1] That charge of "dissembling" is quite intelligible from the subjective
standpoint of Paul, who on questions of religious
principle tolerated no want of consistency and
thoroughness; but looked at objectively, it was
obviously too severe, for it presupposes that Peter
had, against his conscience and better knowledge,
renounced a clearly recognized conviction, whilst
he had really at that time never had such with
regard to this question of the Law. The fail-
ing of Peter was in fact not any moral weakness of character, but defective clearness of view
on a religious matter, which naturally involved as
its consequence indecision in action. Paul himself
proves this by the fact that in censuring Peter he
does not attack any such moral defect as fickleness
or fear of man, but by a dogmatic line of argument
exposes the inconsistency of the Jewish standpoint.
If the adherents of the Law had charged the freer

[1] Gal. ii. 13.

Jewish Christians with having put themselves on
the same level with Gentile sinners, and with having thereby lowered Christ to the place of a servant
of sin, Paul replies to them, that, quite the reverse,
it was they who had done both the Law and Christ
wrong, in seeking to associate them together, instead
of perceiving that the believing Christian has died
with Christ to the Law, that he may henceforth
live only to God.   The Judaists are accordingly
not, as they themselves imagine, the better Christians and full members of the Messianic kingdom,
but, on the contrary, according to Paul's conviction, not true Christians at all as yet, because by
their obdurate adherence to the Law they frus-
trate the divine purpose of the crucifixion of Christ,
and "make void the grace of Christ; for if righteousness comes through the Law, Christ died for
nought."[1]

By this line of argument Paul exposed with
merciless logic the inconsistency of the Judaistic
standpoint, the intrinsic incompatibility of the

---

[1] Gal. ii. 21.

association of faith in Christ with Jewish legalism, and showed that his position of freedom from the Law was not merely to be tolerated, but was the only truly Christian position. But Jewish Christianity was unable to follow him to this conclusion; from this time, therefore, it held aloof from Paul in timid distrust. And as a violation of the conditions of the agreement at Jerusalem was discovered in his consistent abrogation of the Law, that agreement was no longer considered by the Jewish Christians as binding on them, and a course of opposition to the Apostle was commenced within his own Gentile Christian churches. How far the original Apostles personally may have taken part in it is hard to say, since on this point we have no definite information to go upon. When, however, we consider that the Judaizing agitators appealed to the honoured names of the first Apostles, and accredited themselves to the Gentile churches by the production of letters of introduction, which they had undoubtedly brought with them from Palestine, it is hardly conceivable that their action should have been wholly unshared by the first Apostles. Moreover, had that been the case, the tone of irritation in which Paul speaks more than once of "those of repute," the "pillars" and "pre-eminent Apostles," and emphasizes his independence and equality in relation to them, would be hardly intelligible. Still, it must be considered, on the other hand, that in dealing with the parties in Corinth, Paul refrains from all polemical allusion to Peter, whose name one party had made its watchword, that he nowhere attacks the authority of the earlier Apostles, but, on the contrary, acknowledges the priority in time of their apostleship, and calls himself the least of the Apostles, who was not worthy to be called an Apostle, because he persecuted the Church, but who had through the grace of God laboured more than all the rest.[1] The parent church, too, is mentioned in a kindly manner by Paul shortly before his last journey to Jerusalem,[2] the Heathen Christians being described as debtors to the poor saints at Jerusalem : it is true that in the same connection he intimates that he has a slight doubt whether

---

[1] 1 Cor. xv. 9 sq.   [2] Rom. xv. 27.

he and his gift will find a kindly reception in Jerusalem. That this doubt was by no means without foundation is proved by the disastrous issue of his visit, when the Jewish Christian brethren appear, at all events, not to have shown to the sorely pressed Apostle to the Heathen earnest sympathy or active assistance. If we take these various indications into consideration, we may probably conclude that the relation of Paul to the parent church was that of a cool, reserved respect, not unmixed with mistrust and irritation. This becomes the more intelligible if we may suppose that, as previously at the Apostolic Council, so subsequently, two tendencies of thought existed within the parent church itself—the more liberal and tolerant represented by Peter, and the more rigid and exclusive represented by James. Although the latter tendency may, after the occurrence in Antioch, have gained generally the upperhand in Jerusalem, the conciliatory influence of a Peter would nevertheless prevent a complete severance of all relations, and Paul might therefore still continue to cherish the hope of being able, by his personal appearance with the offering of the rich contributions of the Gentile world, to change the feeling of the church of Jerusalem in his favour.

If we now proceed to take a glance at the subsequent phases of this conflict between Paul and Judaism, we must in the first instance direct our attention to the events taking place in *Galatia.* On his second visit to the churches there Paul found their condition had altered much for the worse. Judaizers had appeared in their midst, who had undoubtedly come from elsewhere, from Antioch or Jerusalem, throwing the Heathen Christian churches into commotion and confusion, and representing to them that the adoption of the Jewish Law, at all events of circumcision and the fasts, was the indispensable condition of full Christian salvation. And in so doing they appealed to the authority of the first Apostles and of Barnabas, who had been one of the founders of the churches in Galatia, and, on the other hand, sought to lower that of Paul, describing him as only a disciple of the Apostles, and even throwing doubt on his personal honour. By appearing in person, Paul hoped to allay the storm of Jewish reaction which had been conjured up ; but no sooner had he taken his departure than the hostile intrigues assumed a still more threatening shape. On receiving information of this, Paul wrote his Epistle to the Galatians, that marvellous attestation of Christian liberty, that monument of a religious genius who was many centuries in advance of his age.

He defends in the first instance the independence of his Apostolic authority : he was not called by men to be an Apostle, nor by human tradition did he learn his gospel, but by the immediate revelation of Jesus Christ. To the Jewish principle of authority and tradition he thus places in opposition the evangelical principle of the immediate assurance of divine truth felt in the soul through mysterious contact with the Divine Spirit, which bears within itself the seal of its truth. And this very same experience of an inward revelation of the spirit, wherein lay the source of his knowledge of the gospel, he presupposes as existing also in his readers, and to it he appeals as the supreme rule and test of all religious truth.[1] "This only would I learn from you, Received ye the spirit from works of Law or from the preaching of faith? He therefore that supplied to you the spirit and worketh powers in you, doeth he that by works of Law or by the preaching of faith?" But as the true divine revelation within the soul can never be opposed to the divine revelation in history, Paul immediately adds to the appeal to the Christian consciousness of the Galatians a proof in confirmation from the history of Abraham: inasmuch as faith was counted to Abraham for righteousness, believers are the true children of Abraham; and since in Abraham all Heathen nations are to be blessed, believing Heathen are the true heirs of Abraham's promise. (Paul finds the same truth confirmed also by the fact that the promise was made to "Abraham and his seed," for by this word "seed" in the singular only Christ can be intended.[2] Surprising as the line of argument appears at first sight, the strangeness of it is lessened when we consider that in Paul's view Christ was not a mere individual like

---

[1] Gal. iii. 2, 4.   [2] Gal. iii. 16.

others, but the archetypal Head of the sons of God generally, and thereby the *one* representative of all those for whom the divine promises of grace are intended.) However, his Jewish opponents could object to all this, that really the Law was added to the promise as the condition of sharing the blessing of Abraham, and that therefore faith in Christ would not of itself suffice, but needed to be supplemented by the works of the Law. This objection, in which the vital point of the Jewish Christian position was found, Paul refuted by a double line of argument. He proved first, from the essential relation of law to promise, that they were opposed to each other as mutually exclusive principles, the meritorious *deed* of man and the retributive judgment—the *curse* of God, answering to the Law, and, on the other hand, the *faith* of man without desert and the gift of grace—the *blessing* of God, answering to the promise. He proved next, from the historical relation of the Law to the promise, that it could not form a restrictive condition to the latter; for as a limiting clause may not be added to a valid covenant, so the Law which came in 430 years after, cannot be intended as such a clause, by which God's covenant of promise with Abraham would lose its original character of a gift of grace. Moreover, the promise, he continues, was given directly by God alone, but the Law only indirectly, that is, by the mediation of angels and Moses, a circumstance like-wise indicating the subordinate importance of the latter in comparison with the former. But how can that be? Shall the Law contradict the promise? Paul foresees this objection on the part of his opponents, but he at once parries it by showing that the Law was simply designed to be an instrument to prepare for the fulfilment of the promise, for the very reason that it was unable itself to give life; it was intended to keep men under the captivity of sin until the promise of blessing should be fulfilled by faith in Christ in the case of the spiritual children of Abraham.[1]

With this Paul has defended victoriously his principle of faith against the Galatian Judaizers. He does not stop there, however; but, as in the

---

[1] Gal. iii. 19—25.

contention with Peter in Antioch, passes from the defence to the attack. If his opponents supposed that the Christianity of the Gentiles was complete only when the works of the Law, circumcision, observance of fasts and the like, had been added to faith in Christ, Paul called on them to consider that this supposed completion was, on the contrary, but a lamentable relapse from the religion of the spirit and the truth into that of the flesh, into the service of the miserable and weak elements of nature. He places therefore the ceremonies of the Mosaic Law point-blank upon an equality with those of the Heathen religions, putting both into the common category of nature-worship, with its sense-limitations and absence of spirit and power.[1] He thereby pronounces freedom from the Jewish Law not simply a thing permissible to the Christian, but positively a Christian duty, which the Christian may not surrender, unless he means to lose Christ and fall from grace. "For freedom Christ has set us free; stand fast therefore, and be not

---

[1] Gal. iv. 3, 8 sq.

K

entangled again in a yoke of bondage."[1]   To be circumcised or uncircumcised is of no importance to the Christian, but faith alone which worketh by love; in that is he a new creature; the world has been crucified unto him, the old bondage to the elements of the world has been ended, and its place is taken by the voluntary bondage of the Christian spirit, which addresses God, "Abba, dear Father," and brings the true fulfilment of the Law in self-sacrificing love of the brethren.[2]

The superiority of Christianity to all pre-Christian forms of religion has never been more clearly or grandly declared than is here done by Paul. But that very declaration of superiority involved the magnifying of the difference between it and Judaism into a complete antagonism, into an irrevocable breach.   And Paul did not for a moment shrink from drawing this necessary inference.   For in a remarkable allegorical interpretation of the narrative of Sarah and Hagar and their two sons,[3] he

---

[1] Gal. v. 1 sq.   [2] Gal. v. 6, 13, vi. 14, 15.

[3] Gal. iv. 21—31.

pronounces the Heathen Christians in their freedom from the Law the only true sons of the free mother, the legitimate heirs of the promise according to Isaac; but the legal Jerusalem he describes, on the contrary, as the son of the bond-woman, who may not inherit with the son of the free woman. According to this view, the Gentile Christians are no longer merely the tolerated sharers of the promises of Abraham, but they are the only legitimate heirs, who must take the place of the children of Abraham by natural descent. Accordingly, the pride and consolation of the Jew, that the ancient promises of God belong to his nation, are brought to nought; he may no more have any advantage above the despised Heathen nations; the Law, too, in which he found his highest glory, has been deprived of its value, has been placed on a par with Heathen forms of worship; everything to which the heart of a Jew had for five centuries tenaciously and jealously clung, has been wrested from him and broken up and cast before his feet as a worthless gewgaw. Naturally all Jews and all of the Jewish way of thinking

were indignant at this. We are therefore not
surprised to find the daring Apostle to the Heathen
ever after persecuted wherever he went by his
Judaistic opponents. Still, Paul himself subsequently modified this sternly unconciliatory attitude towards Judaism, as presented in the Epistle
to the Galatians, and sought by a more considerate
and conciliatory attitude again to pacify Jewish
feeling.

Before that could be done, however, Paul had once
more to wage a battle with the same Judaistic opponents, a battle which was the more severe as those
opponents met him on the new field with fresh and
keener weapons. In the church at Corinth, teachers
of Jewish race had appeared from the outside, professing to be " Christ's servants and Apostles," and
this in such a pre-eminent sense, that they employed
against Paul as a party cry the claim "to be Christ's."[1]
These people wished to bring to the Corinthian
Christians another Jesus, another Spirit, and another Gospel than they had received from Paul ;

---

[1] 1 Cor. i. 12: Χριστοῦ εἶναι ; comp. 2 Cor. x. 7.

and they appear, with this claim to be the bearers
of a more excellent Christianity, to have soon
obtained in Corinth such a footing as to have
in the highest degree astonished and incensed
Paul, because he then felt the ground giving way
under his feet in the chief city of Greece even.
They were the old opponents again, and it was
therefore naturally the old quarrel which re-appeared in this disturbance in Corinth.   But the
method of warfare was different, and the immediate
points of attack had been more skilfully selected
than in Galatia.   These Corinthian agitators did not
disturb the pleasure-loving and enlightened Greeks
with the requirement of circumcision and other
Jewish ceremonial observances, but they directed
their assault this time immediately against the very
centre of the Pauline Gospel.   Paul, they said to
the Corinthians, had not preached to them the true
Christ, whom he, in fact, did not himself know,
as he had never seen or heard him; they, on the
other hand, who had themselves seen and heard
Jesus, and had had personal intercourse with him
and his immediate disciples, could preach to them

the true Jesus and the only true gospel of the
Messianic kingdom.[1]   In contrast with the Pauline
Christ, the Son of God according to the spirit,
they set up " Christ according to the flesh," as
Paul says, that is, the Jesus of history as present
to the memory of the First Church, and according
to his outward appearance a Jew loyal to the Law.
Accordingly their gospel of the Messianic kingdom
was also another than Paul's : not the gospel of the
spirit which quickeneth, but of the letter which
killeth ; or, when they did speak of a " spirit,"
it was not the spirit of the new covenant, the
radiant glory of which had been revealed in the
soul of Paul, but the spirit of the old covenant, the
glory of which was transient, the spirit of Moses,
which is the servile spirit of fear.   To "enslave"
the Corinthian Christians under this rigid Jewish
spirit had therefore been the object of the Judaizers
in this case also; only the way to this object was
different from that taken previously in Galatia; it
was no longer the direct authority of Moses and

---

[1] 2 Cor. xi. 4.

Jewish tradition which was brought into the field against the free and spiritual gospel of Paul, but in the first instance that of Jesus and primitive Apostolic tradition.

The situation of Paul was thereby rendered still more perilous; for to a superficial judgment, such as that of most men ordinarily is, the weakness of his authority lay undoubtedly in the circumstance that he had not been a disciple of the historical Jesus, and was not able to base his Apostolic call upon a fact that could be outwardly perceived and acknowledged. The fight about the question of the principle of Paul's gospel assumed therefore in this case the form of a personal struggle as to the legitimacy of Paul's Apostleship. And this struggle became for Paul the more dangerous as his enemies did not shrink from the most offensive means of humiliating and discrediting him. As, in order not to be burdensome to the Church, he had foregone all claim to support and had earned his livelihood by the labour of his hands, his opponents discovered therein an implicit admission on his part that he had no right to come forward as an Apostle and to

make an Apostle's claims on the Church.[1]   When
he zealously collected the charitable offerings for
the poor church at Jerusalem, they laid against
him the base charge of seeking to obtain by stealthy
methods what he did not dare to attempt openly,
and of filling his own pockets at the expense of the
Corinthians.[2] When he appealed to his deepest and
most secret experiences, to his sight of Jesus as the
glorified Lord from heaven, to his other "revelations and visions" in which he was caught away
into the third heaven, he was pronounced out of his
mind, and said to be always boasting of himself.[3]
Indeed, even the endless afflictions which he had to
endure for the Gospel's sake, seem to have been
interpreted to his disadvantage as a mark of divine
disfavour.[4] Is it to be wondered at that, in view of
such malicious attacks, the feelings of Paul should
have been passionately stirred, that he should call

---

[1] 1 Cor. ix.; 2 Cor. xi. 7 sq., xii. 13.

[2] 2 Cor. xii. 16 sq., viii. 20, 21.

[3] 2 Cor. v. 13, xii. 1—13.

[4] 2 Cor. i. 5 sq., iv. 7 sq., vi. 4 sq., xi. 23 sq.

his opponents "lying Apostles" and "servants of
Satan," who only fashion themselves as servants of
righteousness?[1] It was to him a question of life or
death, and his situation was an extremely difficult
one. What had he to oppose to the weapons of his
opponents? No testimonials from human authorities, no letters of commendation from Jerusalem;
nothing but the testimony of his conscience and
the letter of commendation furnished him by God
himself, an epistle supplied in the actual results of
his work, in the very existence of the Corinthian
church.[2] " Our glorying is this, the testimony
of our conscience, that in holiness and sincerity of
God, not in fleshly wisdom but in the grace of
God, we behaved ourselves in the world, and more
abundantly to you-ward;" " Our epistle are ye,
written in our hearts, known and read of all
men;" " In everything commending ourselves as
the servants of God, in much patience, in afflictions, in necessities, in long suffering and kindness,
in holy spirit, in love unfeigned, in the word of

---

[1] 2 Cor. xi. 13, 14.   [2] 2 Cor. i. 12, iii. 2, vi. 4 sq.

truth, in the power of God, by the weapons of righteousness, defensive and offensive, by honour and dishonour, by evil report and good report, as deceivers and yet true, as unknown and yet known, as dying, and, behold, we live, as chastened and yet not killed, as sorrowful but alway rejoicing, as poor yet making many rich, as having nothing and yet possessing all things! O ye Corinthians, our mouth is open unto you, our heart is enlarged, but ye are straitened in your own heart—I speak as to my children—do ye the same to me, and be ye also enlarged!"

And such affectionate entreaty and admonition the Corinthians could not in truth resist. While he was on the way to Corinth, Paul received through Titus, whom he had sent on before him, the most assuring reports of a happy turn in the feeling of the majority of the church, who were seeking by redoubled zeal to atone for the wrong which they had done the beloved Apostle. And we may infer with great probability from the tone and feeling of the *Epistle to the Romans*, which was being written during this stay in Corinth, that his

appearance there immediately afterwards smoothed
the agitated waves of party strife at last, that
a mutual approach and reconciliation of the contending interests was initiated, which exercised also
a certain reactive effect on the feeling of the Apostle
himself and his way of looking at things. The
Epistle to the Romans is distinguished from all the
other Epistles of the Apostle's by its calm and
objective character and decidedly conciliatory purpose, the reason of which must be sought partly in
the mood of the writer at the time, and partly in
the peculiar circumstances of the church in Rome.

That church had not been founded by Paul, and
had not, down to that time, stood in any personal
relation to him; nor, according to all appearances,
were there any anti-Pauline agitators in it; in its
tone of thought the church was generally rather
inclined towards the Apostle of the Heathen than
against him, for he repeatedly acknowledges its
condition to have been praiseworthy.[1] But it was
composed of Jews and Gentiles, and the mutual

---

[1] Rom. i. 8—12, vi. 17, xv. 14.

relations of these two sections were evidently so
strained that its healthy development was daily
placed in greater peril, and the more so as through
the rapid growth of the Heathen section, the
Jewish, which had undoubtedly formed the principal original element, sunk into the position of
a powerless minority.   The arrogance of many
Roman Gentile Christians, their offensive want of
consideration for their despised Jewish brethren,
together with their heathenish frivolity in moral
conduct, was naturally but little adapted to reconcile the Jewish Christian section to a turn of
things which was to them so puzzling and incomprehensible.   This growingly Gentile Messianic
kingdom was as contrary to their Jewish hopes as
it was to their strictly legal principles of life.   Having been thus grieved and deceived in their most
sacred relations, probably not a few may have with-
drawn offended from their Gentile brethren and
returned to the Synagogue, so that the unity of the
church was in serious danger of being broken up.
Such a condition of the Roman church is implied,
I believe, in the Epistle to the Romans itself,

when we duly consider all the hints it contains.
It is not my business to place before you on this
occasion the rich contents of this Epistle, as to do
that I should have to re-state the whole doctrinal
system of the Apostle which occupied us in the last
Lecture. Allow me to direct your special attention
further only to those points in which Paul has
distinctly qualified his anti-Judaistic position in
the interests of a peaceful reconciliation with the
Jewish-Christian habit of thought, thereby preparing
for the development of a common Catholic form of
doctrine.

In general, the endeavour, which appears in this
Epistle much more decidedly than before, to connect
the Pauline Gospel with the Old Testament and to
show that it is a fulfilment of prophecy,[1] is of itself
worthy of remark. Coming to details, the modifi-
cation may be observed in the three main articles of
Paul's previous controversies—his doctrine of Christ,
of the Law, and of the hope of Israel. In opposition to the Corinthian "Christ party," Paul had
laid great stress on the idealism of his Christology:

---

[1] E.g. Rom. i. 2, 17, iii. 21, 31, iv. 1—25, vii. 1, ix. 6, 25—
29, 33, x. 5—21, xiii. 9, xv. 8—12.

"The Lord is the Spirit; although we had known Christ after the flesh, henceforth we know him no more (that is, in that way)." Subsequently, after closer intercourse with the moderate Jewish Christians (the Petrine section), he may have arrived at the conviction that the historical realism which attaches importance to the terrestrial personality of Jesus has after all a legitimate side, and he may have felt this the more readily as by it a salutary counterpoise was supplied to the spiritual transcendentalism of the followers of Apollos. In the Epistle to the Romans we find him, accordingly, now combining this historic and realistic way of regarding things with his own idealistic tendencies in such a manner as to put the former into the foreground, making it heighten by contrast the effect of the latter: thus by the flesh Christ is undoubtedly the son of David, but by the spirit of holiness the Son of God; by the flesh he sprang from the Fathers of Israel and belongs therefore peculiarly to the Jewish nation, but at the same time he is the Divine Lord who is above all, whether Jews or Heathen.[1]

---

[1] Rom. i. 3, 4, ix. 5, xv. 8.

Further, as regards the Law, in the Epistle to the Galatians Paul had placed it, as far as its ritualistic portions were concerned, on a level with Heathen nature-worship, and had summarily denominated the legal system a " curse," in antithesis to the spirit of Christ. But now he energetically protests against the idea that he deems the Law itself carnal and impure, or a principle of sin; on the contrary, he regards ɔ as in itself spiritual and holy, righteous and good, and the cause of its disastrous effects lies simply in the carnal nature of man.[1] Nor does he now go so far as to pronounce adherence to the laws regarding feast-days and food nothing less than a falling away from Christ, as he had done in the Epistle to the Galatians, but concedes that the legally scrupulous, or " the weak," may observe their abstentions and practices to the Lord; he pronounces such things, therefore, *adiaphora*, with regard to which every one may consult his own conscience, and not in themselves reprehensible and unchristian; indeed, he makes it quite a duty on the part of

---

[1] Rom. vii. 7—14, viii. 3.

those of freer views, or "the strong," to observe
an indulgent and kind consideration and tolerance
towards the weak.[1] This remarkable change may
find its explanation in two causes: first, in the
circumstances of the Roman church, in which just
then the legalists no longer played the part of
assailants and oppressors, but of the assailed and
oppressed; next, probably in the personal experiences of Paul at Corinth, where he could not avoid
perceiving that the legal way of thinking followed
by the moderate Jewish Christians really had a very
healthy side worthy of all consideration, whilst the
Gentile-Christian freedom from the Law in many
instances sunk in moral worth in proportion as, in
an arrogant over-estimate of its own importance, it
boasted of its advanced illumination. The traces of
experiences of this kind may be plainly perceived in
the practical admonitions of the Epistle to the Romans,
which supply us not merely with guidance for the
understanding of the state of the church at Rome,
but also give us acceptable information as regards

---

[1] Rom. xiv. and xv.

the state of things which had arisen in Corinth after Paul's last arrival there: these traces show a reaction amongst the extreme parties, an internal approximation of the disciples of Peter and of Paul to a standpoint of general church union.

This irenic tendency, finally, may be observed most distinctly in the case of the third of the Apostle's former standpoints. In the Epistle to the Galatians Paul had gone so far as to declare the children of Abraham by natural descent—that is, the people of Israel—outcast, the disinherited children of the bondwoman, and that by the spiritual children of Abraham from the free woman—that is, the believing Heathen—who are alone legitimate heirs. And this harsh utterance appeared from year to year to be more and more terribly confirmed by the actual results of his mission, which gave a severe shock to the Jewish Christians, who could not easily forget that the Messiah Jesus had himself sprung from Israel, and that it was Israel's promises which must be fulfilled in his kingdom. And Paul was the less able to deny the justice of this doubt, inasmuch as he himself painfully shared the patriotic grief at the unbelief of Israel. In the discussion of this point (Rom. ix.) he accordingly strikes quite another key than that of the Epistle to the Galatians. He assures the disheartened Jewish Christians in Rome of his intense sympathy with his own people, to whom belong the adoption and the glory and the covenants and the giving of the Law, and the service of God and the promises, whose are the Fathers, and of whom Christ came according to the flesh. On that account God's word of promise to this people cannot have wholly come to nought. " God hath not cast off his people which he foreknew," Paul says now, and thereby directly retracts the hard utterance about the "casting out" of the children of Abraham by natural descent.[1] Israel has stumbled indeed at the stone of offence, the cross of Christ and righteousness by faith, yet not that it might fall and remain fallen for ever, but only that it might make possible the entrance of the Heathen into the Messianic kingdom ; and when Israel's loss has brought about

---

[1] Rom. xi. 2 ; comp. Gal. iv. 30.

the riches of the Gentiles, then the fulness of the Gentiles will in return provoke Israel to emulation. Israel's present unbelief does not therefore mean its final rejection by God, but only its temporary putting back, in order to promote God's plan of universal salvation, which will find its ultimate end in the reception of all into the Divine favour. True, the first have become last and the last first; the natural branches of the olive of Israel have been cut out to make room for the wild offshoot of the Heathen; but the latter may not on that account glory unfeelingly over Israel, but must remember that God can also cut them out again and graft Israel in once more.[1] Thus the Pauline universalism, which seemed at first only to turn against Israel, in this Epistle undergoes a change in favour of Israel: the object of it was to console and encourage those who had been put back, to humble and warn those who had been put first, and thus to unite all alike in the brotherly unity of the new Church of the all-embracing kingdom of God, in which there is

---

[1] Rom. xi. 18—24.

no more Jew or Greek. This was the ripest fruit of the conflicts between the Apostle to the Gentiles and the Jewish Christians; and this was at the same time the testament which Paul left to the nascent Universal Church.

LECTURE IV.

THE RECONCILIATION OF PAULINISM AND JEWISH
CHRISTIANITY.

THE RECONCILIATION OF PAULINISM AND JEWISH CHRISTIANITY.

In the last Lecture I endeavoured to put before you a sketch of the conflicts of the Apostle Paul with Jewish Christianity. We saw how they took their rise in the occurrences at Antioch, reached their climax in the proceedings of the Galatian and Corinthian churches, and how, after the victory over the Corinthian opponents, the intense strain in the relations of the parties gave place to that milder tone and conciliatory bearing of which the Epistle to the Romans supplies evidence. And the continuance of this pacific tone of feeling at the time of the Roman imprisonment of the Apostle can be gathered from the *Epistle to the Philippians*, which was written from Rome. Paul has, it is true, to complain in this Epistle also of personal opponents,[1] who preach Christ, of envy and strife, with secret motives of ill-will against him; but he nevertheless allows, in the case of these opponents, that they really preach Christ, and he even rejoices at their work, because it serves, after all, the common cause. How very unlike his severe condemnation of those Galatian and Corinthian opponents, who proclaimed another Jesus and another gospel than his, is this mild, tolerant tone! But the question rises: "Is this change of judgment to be traced solely to the personal feeling of the Apostle, and not also to the circumstance that the Jewish Christians as a fact no longer put another Jesus in opposition to the Pauline Christ, but on this central point of his gospel drew nearer to him, learnt from him, and agreed with him?" The very tone of the Epistles to the Romans and the Philippians suggests the conjecture that on Roman soil a softening of the differences and the initiation of a conciliatory movement had from the first taken

---

[1] Phil. i. 15—18.

place. And a confirmation of this conjecture may be found, as it seems to me, in that book of the New Testament which was the first from the Jewish Christian side and written only a few years after the Apostle to the Gentiles had left the scene of his earthly labours. I refer to the *Apocalypse of John.*

It is now pretty generally acknowledged that the date of this book is the year 68-69 A.D.; but I cannot consider it probable that the Apostle John, as is still commonly supposed, was its author. It is not merely that the writer nowhere calls himself an "Apostle," but he speaks[1] of the twelve Apostles with such objectivity that he cannot well himself be of their number; indeed, he appears to pre-suppose their death as already an accomplished fact.[2] There is, further, the special consideration that the description of the judgment upon the city of Rome, Rev. xviii., decidedly produces the impression that it is an *eye-witness* of the reign of terror in the days of the Neronian conflagration and the following persecution of the Christians who is speaking. For these reasons I consider it in the highest degree

---

[1] Rev. xxi. 14.　　　[2] Rev. xviii. 20.

probable that the author of the Apocalypse was a Jewish Christian of Rome, who had come into Asia Minor, perhaps in his flight from the Neronian persecution (A.D. 64), had made the acquaintance of the churches there, and now, when the fall of Jerusalem was approaching, turned his prophetic eye both in that direction and also towards Rome, so that the burning recollection of the days of terror in Rome under Nero became in his mind the symbol of the coming judgment upon the proud and sinful Babylon.   If this supposition is, as I do not doubt, correct, it follows from it that the author of the Apocalypse must, as a member of the church of Rome during the years 62—64, have had personal relations with the Apostle Paul ; and inasmuch as a man so eminent as the author of the Apocalypse in any case was, will certainly have played a prominent part as a leader of his party, we have every reason for supposing that he occupied a place in the front rank of those Jewish Christians in Rome of whom Paul, partly complaining of and partly acknowledging them, gives his opinion in the Epistle to the Philippians.   Paul there brings the charge against his opponents that their Christian labours are not free from envy, from secret selfish intentions and ill-will towards himself; indeed, that they even seek to render his situation still worse and more painful than it is.[1] And no doubt they did this by making his principle of freedom from the Law, and with it himself, responsible for the moral excesses of the Heathen Christians, a representation which naturally produced a prejudicial influence upon the course of his trial. At the same time, he acknowledges with rejoicing that, in spite of all this, these opponents really preach Christ, who must have been, therefore, the Christ of his gospel, that Lord who is the spirit, and not merely a "Christ according to the flesh," such as the Corinthian Judaists had put forward in opposition to the Pauline Christ according to the spirit. Paul therefore recognizes a spiritual faith in Christ as the uniting bond between himself and his Roman opponents, whilst all along their envy at his success, their suspicion of his principle of freedom from the Law—in a word, their Judaic prejudices and intrigues against himself—continued to exist.

---

[1] Phil. i. 15—18.

When we inspect more closely the relation of the author of the Apocalypse to Paul, we meet with essentially the same features as were presented by the Apostle's Roman opponents. It is especially clear that the author is personally not favourably disposed towards Paul. He beholds,[1] written on the foundation-walls of the new Jerusalem, the names of the twelve Apostles, the representatives of the twelve tribes of Israel; for the Apostle of the Gentiles there is no room. In fact, whether he recognizes him as an Apostle at all, is left in ambiguous obscurity. The language used to the church at Ephesus suggests the conclusion that he did not. It is true that when this church is commended[2] because it could not bear those which were "evil," and had tried and found liars those which professed to be Apostles and were not, and because it hated the works of the Nicolaitanes, whom Christ also hated, we must suppose that in the first instance such Paulinists are intended who, appealing to the authority of Paul, perverted his principle of liberty ("all

---

[1] Rev. xxi. 14.   [2] Rev. ii. 2, 6.

things are lawful," "all things are clean," "the earth is the Lord's and the fulness thereof"[1]) into a pretext for indulging the liberty of the flesh,[2] the continuation of Heathen practices and vices, such as participation in the sacrificial feasts of Heathen gods and the practice of unchastity.[3] But the important point is, that Paul himself had pronounced quite another judgment on these things; that he had again and again most emphatically condemned Heathen levity of this description on the part of his professed disciples (" Ye cannot partake of the table of the Lord and of the table of demons;" "Flee fornication! or know ye not that your body is a temple of the holy spirit, which ye have from God, and are not your own?"[4]); and that this is so completely ignored by the author, that his readers must

---

[1] 1 Cor. vi. 12, x. 26 ; Rom. xiv. 20.

[2] Comp. Gal. v. 13 ; Rom. vi. 1.

[3] Rev. ii. 14, 20. (To suppose that "mixed marriages" only are intended by πορνεῦσαι, is, I consider, an entirely arbitrary limitation of the general meaning, for which no justification is supplied either in the immediate connection or in analogous cases : comp. 1 Cor. v. 1, vi.)

[4] 1 Cor. x. 21, vi. 12—20; Rom. xiii. 13 ; 1 Thess. iv. 3 sq., &c.

almost of necessity get the impression that with those "evil" ones and false Apostles, not merely the licentious Paulinists but Paul himself was meant to be condemned. In this, however, the author of the Apocalypse betrays the vice which, according to the experience of all ages, party feeling ever brings with it, of not distinguishing between a principle and its abuse, and of charging the excesses of individual opponents upon a whole party, and especially its leaders, however innocent the latter may be. This was another instance of the Jewish party tactics which Paul had previously had to complain of at Rome, as we saw above from indications in the Epistle to the Philippians.

But we find in the Apocalypse none the less the idealistic conception of Christ which Paul acknowledged in Rome as the bond of union between himself and his opponents there. Like the Pauline Christology, that of the author of the Apocalypse hinges on the one hand on the expiatory death, and on the other on the celestial glory of Christ, whilst the earthly life of Jesus is referred to only so far that Christ is called the "Offspring of David" and the "Lion of Juda;" just as Paul in the Epistle to the Romans had connected Christ's descent from David with his Divine Sonship. As Paul denominated Christ the Passover slain for us, so our author likes to describe him as "the Lamb slain for us," and finds in his violent death a proof of his love for us and an expiation to purify us from the guilt of sin, a ransom to redeem us to God.[1] Again, as Paul calls Christ the first fruits of them that slept, so in the Apocalypse we find him termed the first-born from the dead.[2] As, according to Paul, Christ has been exalted to the regal dignity of divine dominion over all, so, according to our author, he has taken his seat on the throne by the side of his Father, participating therefore in His divine dominion and power; he is the Lord of the churches, holds their stars, or guardian angels, in his hand, and is also Ruler of nations and King of kings, the all-wise and almighty Judge of the nations; indeed, to him is due a worship similar to that of God himself.[3] As the author of the Apocalypse in his

---

[1] Rev. i. 5, vii. 14, v. 9.   [2] Rev. i. 5 ; comp. 1 Cor. xv. 20.

[3] Rev. i. 5, iii. 21, ii. 12, 16, 23, v. 8—14, xi. 15, xix. 16, xx. 6.

apotheosis of Christ as an object of worship thus
almost outstrips Paul, neither does he in his dogmatic definitions of Christ's nature at all fall behind
the Apostle.   Like Paul, he calls Christ the " Son
of God" in the metaphysical sense of a god-like spiritual being, and far beyond the merely theocratic significance of the title.   As Paul had said, " The Lord
is the Spirit," so our author identifies Christ with
the Spirit, or celestial principle of revelation which
speaks to the churches and rules in them.[1]   As Paul
had had a vision of Christ as the Man from heaven
in celestial light and glory, so the author of the
Apocalypse likewise beholds him in a super-mun-
dane form like unto a son of man, his face shining
as the sun.[2]   As Paul had described the celestial
Son of Man as at the same time the image of God,
the agent of creation, the head of every man, and
finally even God over all,[3] so the Christ of the
Apocalypse introduces himself with the predicates

---

[1] Rev. ii. 7, xi. 18.

[2] Rev. i. 13, xiv. 14; comp. 2 Cor. iii. 17, 18, iv. 4, 6; 1 Cor.
xv. 47.

[3] 1 Cor. viii. 6, xi. 3; Rom. ix. 5.

of Divine majesty, " I am the Alpha and the Omega, saith the Lord God, who is and who was and who is to come, the All-powerful;"[1] and he is accordingly called[2] also " the Head of creation" and " the Word of God," that is, the mediating instrument of all divine revelation from the creation of the world to the final judgment.

It appears from this that the similarity of the Christology of the Apocalypse to that of Paul is complete; this Christ occupies the same exalted position as the Pauline Christ above the terrestrial Son of Man. Would such a view of Christ be conceivable in the case of a man who had lived in personal intercourse with Jesus? I think we have in this another proof that the author of the Apocalypse was not the Apostle John. But if he was a Jewish Christian of Rome, no doubt can exist as to the source of his Christology; its intrinsic likeness to the Pauline form of doctrine betrays its direct

---

[1] Rev. i. 8, xxii. 13. (From this parallelism and the connection with i. 7, it appears to me that the reference of i. 8 to Christ is placed beyond doubt.)

[2] Rev. iii. 14, ἀρχὴ τῆς κτίσεως ; xix. 13, ὁ λόγος τοῦ θεοῦ.

origin in Pauline influences.   Supposing that to be
the case, we can the more readily understand how
Paul could truly rejoice at the proclamation of Christ
by his opponents in Rome, in spite of all their
unfriendliness towards himself personally : he really
saw his opponents walking in his own footsteps.
The power of genius in history is just this, that it
compels its very enemies against their will to submit
to, to learn from, and to serve it.   As a fact, the
author of the Apocalypse became the most efficient
herald of the Pauline idea of Christ, by throwing it
into the poetic form of prophetic intuition, in which
it impressed itself on the Greek and Roman no less
than on the Hebrew mind.   Thereby the centre of
cohesion, offering points for the harmonious combination of different theological conceptions, had been
supplied to the contending parties of primitive
Christianity, just when they appeared to be threatened with perpetual disunion in the matter of the
validity of the Law.

The results of this consensus with regard to the
cardinal question of Christology are evident in the
case of the author of the Apocalypse himself in his

more moderate tone in relation to the question of
the Law. Strictly Jewish as his own line of thought
is, and thoroughly suspicious as he is of the idealistic Pauline principle of freedom from the Law,
which he saw degenerating into a heathenish license
of the flesh, he is very far, nevertheless, from the
overbearing intolerance of the zealots of the Law at
Antioch or in Galatia. Nowhere does he put forward the requirement of circumcision, or of the
observance of the Jewish festivals; on the contrary,
to the moderate party of Heathen Christians at
Thyatira, who did not, like the radical libertines
with their cultus of the flesh, think they were
obliged to sound "the depths of Satan," he expressly
declares that he will lay upon them no further
burden, only they must hold fast to their past good
practice.[1] What that was he does not, it is true,
expressly state, but he enables us to gather it with
probability from the antithesis to the evil practices
censured and the other exhortations of the epistles
in the Apocalypse: it was abstinence from all

---

[1] Rev. ii. 24, 25.

Heathen worship and Heathen unchastity—nothing else, therefore, than the simple fundamental principle of pure religion and morality, which had previously always been required of Jewish proselytes, and subsequently of Gentile Christians. To those Heathen Christians who hold fast to this simple principle of Christian morals, and also keep the word and the works of Christ—that is, maintain their Christian confession and life—in faithfulness unto death in the midst of persecution and suffering, the author of the Apocalypse promises the crown of life and a place at the marriage-feast of the Lamb, and a share in Christ's universal dominion, whilst he condemns those Jews who are enemies of Christ as false Jews and of Satan's synagogue.[1] Our author has accordingly got decidedly beyond the narrow limits of Jewish particularism, although it must be allowed that he does not as yet quite occupy the elevation of Pauline universalism, inasmuch as, like the prophets, he still finds in Israel the fundamental element of the theocracy, to which the number of

---

[1] Rev. ii. 9, iii. 9.

Heathen of all nations come as clients and partial citizens permitted to share its privileges.[1] Nevertheless, he recognizes in these multitudes from the Heathen true Christian brethren, "who have washed their robes and made them white in the blood of the Lamb," and whom "the Lamb will feed and guide to the fountains of living water." Paul had similarly written to the Corinthians, that they had washed themselves and been sanctified and justified in the name of the Lord Jesus Christ and in the spirit of our God. In his recognition of the cleansing virtue of faith in Christ for all, including the Gentiles, our Jewish-Christian author, therefore, agrees entirely with Paul; but at the same time, it must be admitted, he pre-supposes that those who are invited to the marriage of the Lamb have been clothed in that silk wedding-garment which consists of the "righteous acts of the saints."[2] The righteousness of the works (of the Law) is, and remains

---

[1] Rev. vii. 3—8, and 9—17, also xix. 5, οἱ μικροί.

[2] Rev. xix. 8, τὰ δικαιώματα τῶν ἁγίων = מִצְוֹת, i. e. acts of obedience to the Law, legally prescribed acts.

in his view, the indispensable condition of participation in the Messianic salvation, and on this realistic standard of moral action he lays the greater stress as he saw the idealism of righteousness by faith going in practice dangerously astray in the case of many Paulinists.

Exactly the same position is taken in this matter by the author of the *Epistle of James*, who in other respects occupies a place further removed from Paul than that of the author of the Apocalypse, inasmuch as, unlike the latter, he lets us catch no glimpse of the Pauline Christology. And while the author of the Apocalypse nowhere directly and expressly opposes Paul himself, it can hardly be doubted that the author of the Epistle of James has done this. His attack upon the Pauline doctrine of justification may, it is true, have had its immediate provocation in the conduct of those Paulinists who, with genuine Greek intellectualism, emptied the Pauline idea of faith of its deep inward meaning, converting it into a doctrine of faith, a dogma, a formula of a creed, a philosophical doctrine of the schools, or, in a word, into a mere matter of the understanding;

thereby throwing into the background at one and
the same time both the religious mysticism and the
moral power of faith in the genuine Pauline sense.
Although this may be accepted as the most probable
occasion of the Epistle of James, there is no room
on that account to doubt that James failed to distinguish between the disfigured doctrine of faith held
by these Paulinists and Paul's own idea of it; undoubtedly he himself understood the latter in the
sense of the former, and thus in his attack on the
disciples of Paul dealt blows at their master at
the same time. When James says, "Ye see that
by works a man is justified, and not only by faith,"[1]
no unprejudiced reader can fail to see in these words
a direct polemical reference to the sentence of Paul,
"We reckon therefore that a man is justified by
faith apart from the works of the Law." Neither
can it well be an accidental coincidence that each
of them produces proof of his position from the
history of Abraham. While Paul sees in the believer
in Christ a new creature that has received the quick-

---

[1] James ii. 24 = Rom. iii. 28.

ening spirit from God, and feels its power as the impulse of love which brings with it the fulfilling of the Law, James considers that faith as such is something dead and powerless, a body without soul, requiring therefore to be first animated and supplemented by works. To a dead faith of this kind, which even the demons may have, Paul would certainly not have promised justification as its fruit; he would, however, not have acknowledged it as genuine faith at all in the Christian sense.

The ground of this contention lies therefore, in the first instance, in a misconception of the nature of faith, or, to speak more definitely, in the fact that James did not comprehend the religious depth of the Pauline idea of faith, any more than that of the Pauline Christology. The further and deeper ground of the contention must be sought in the dissimilarity of the natures of the two men: the mystical inwardness and idealistic speculative bent of Paul's genius was met in the person of James by the sober realism of the practical understanding, which attaches exclusive importance to the uprightness of moral conduct, but is indifferent, or indeed suspicious, with regard to the emotions and intuitions of the religious nature. We certainly may not refuse to this standpoint its relative legitimacy, but must grant that, in the case of many people, and people deserving of all respect, it is one which approves itself again and again as most intelligible and most suited to their natures; indeed, we must go further and allow that it even offers a very valuable counterpoise to the dangers of a barren dogmatism and sectarian orthodoxy, or, what is still worse, of an immoral antinomianism and libertinism, which, as the experience of all ages teaches, may so easily spring out of the excessive emphasizing of faith. At the same time it is certain that, with James as its pioneer, Christianity would never have become a universal religion, nor, indeed, a religion at all distinct from Judaism; just as little as a man like Erasmus could have produced the Reformation of the sixteenth century. The creative forces of religious history are, after all, always such religious heroes as Paul and Luther, who in the depths of their souls have had living experience of the mystery of religion, and have

gazed with the eagle-eye of genius into the deep
things of Deity.

The further reconciliation of the opposition between Paulinism and Jewish Christianity, which
still meets us in the Epistle of James in un-
mitigated intensity, was accomplished partly in
the field of theological Gnosticism, to which the
Alexandrine religious system contributed new in-
gredients of sufficient combining power to unite the
resisting elements, and partly and specially in the
field of Gospel narrative. And in this latter field
the church at Rome was from the very first the
leading spirit. According to ecclesiastical tradition,
the oldest of our Gospels was written in Rome by
Mark, a disciple of the Apostle Peter, after the
death of Peter and Paul.[1] Doubt may be raised,
for one reason or another, it is true, against the
opinion that the author of our second Gospel was an
immediate disciple of Peter and wrote down Peter's
discourses "exactly" (as Papias related); neither
can the mention of Mark in the First Epistle of

---

[1] Eusebius, *Ecc. Hist.* iii. 39, ii. 15 ; Irenæus, *Adv. Hær.* iii. 1.

Peter (v. 13) be considered decisive evidence for
that opinion, since it is conceivable that this very
mention of Mark gave rise to the tradition which
brought him into connection with Peter.   There is
no reason, on the other hand, for doubting that
Mark was found in the immediate society of Paul
during his imprisonment in Rome.[1]   There is, in
fact, very much to be said in favour of ascribing
our second Gospel to this disciple of Paul; for it
exhibits plainly various traces of Pauline influences
and reminiscences.

The sentence at the very opening, in which Mark
summarizes the subject of the preaching of Jesus,
"The time is fulfilled and the kingdom of God is
at hand; repent ye and believe in the gospel!"
reminds us of specifically Pauline forms of expression.[2]   The Evangelist then begins his account of
the labours of Jesus with a series of wonderful cures
and polemical discourses of Jesus, in which from
the very commencement the profound contrast be-

---

[1] Philem. ver. 24 ; Col. iv. 10, 11 ; 2 Tim. iv. 11.

[2] Mark i. 15 ; comp. Gal. iv. 4, iii. 26.

tween the free spirit of the Gospel and the narrow legalism of Judaism finds marked expression. On occasion of a cure on the Sabbath he makes Jesus utter the great sentence, "The Sabbath is for man, and not man for the Sabbath; so that the Son of Man is Lord even of the Sabbath;"[1] a sentence the direct parallel of which does not occur in the other Gospels, whilst the affinity between it and the Pauline declaration, "The Lord is the Spirit, and where the Spirit of the Lord is there is liberty," is obvious. It is not by any means intended by this to raise a doubt as to whether the historical Jesus actually gave utterance to principles of this description; on the contrary, it is in the highest degree probable that he did; but in proportion as the Jewish spirit of the church in Palestine lacked the power to appreciate the reformatory opposition of Jesus to Judaism, the more important was it in the interests of Christianity that the Evangelist Mark had his eyes opened and trained in the school of the Apostle Paul to see what was new in principle in the mission

---

[1] Mark ii. 27, 28; comp. 2 Cor. iii. 17.

and teaching of Jesus. The doctrine of the predestination to salvation of some and the hardening of
others (of the Jewish nation), so characteristic of
Paul, occurs in Mark likewise in genuine Pauline
phraseology.[1] And it is specially indicative of the
Pauline Evangelist that he takes the very words
which Paul had used in his Epistle to the Romans
of the obduracy of the unbelieving Jews generally,
and puts them into the mouth of Jesus as he complains of the want of faith and understanding displayed by his disciples, whom the Evangelist is
never weary of placing, whenever an occasion offers,
in the most unfavourable light imaginable.[2] He
gives special prominence to their dulness and perplexity with regard to the two cardinal articles of
the Pauline gospel—the word of the Cross and of
the resurrection of Jesus. Although Jesus, as the
Evangelist emphatically insists, "spoke the saying
(of his death and resurrection) openly and unreserv-
edly," ($\pi\alpha\rho\rho\eta\sigma\iota\alpha$), they remained, notwithstanding,

---

[1] Mark x. 40, iv. 11, 12 ; comp. Rom. ix. 23, xi. 8.

[2] Mark viii. 17, 18, ix. 19.

in ignorance with regard to it, and, in timid embarrassment, did not venture to question him about it;[1] for they, and especially Peter, minded not the things of God, but the things of men. Similarly, when Jesus, after his transfiguration, spoke of the resurrection of the Son of Man, the disciples, as Mark relates, questioned among themselves, in perplexity, what the rising from the dead should mean.[2] Now, though criticism may raise doubts as to the historical character of these definite predictions of death and resurrection, it is at all events certain that *if* on some occasion Jesus spoke thus openly on the point, as the Evangelist reports, the persistent inability on the part of the disciples to understand such utterances would be very hard to comprehend. We shall therefore be obliged to see in this language of the Evangelist at least a strong hyperbole, the cause of which will have to be sought in his general estimate of the first Apostles.

---

[1] Mark viii. 32, 33, ix. 32; comp. 1 Cor. ii. 14, 15; Rom. x. 2, 3; 2 Cor. iv. 4.

[2] Mark ix. 10.

When, now, we consider that it was precisely the perception of the meaning of the death and resurrection of Christ that formed the basis of the Pauline system, what the Evangelist meant is clear when he thus pointedly emphasized the inability of the disciples to understand those cardinal points of the Pauline gospel. It is just here also that we may find the clue for deciphering the hieroglyphic of the narrative of the transfiguration; for it is quite obvious that this is an idealistic narrative, for which the Apocalypse and the Pauline Christology have supplied the elements. Just as Paul placed the imperishable glory of God in the face of Christ in contrast with the transient glory on the face of Moses, and inferred thence the inferiority and transient significance of the old covenant of the letter as compared with the surpassing and permanent glory of the new covenant of the Gospel of the Spirit;[1] in like manner the allegorical narrative of the Evangelist places the transfigured Jesus side by side with the two representatives of the old

---

[1] 2 Cor. iii. 7—11, iv. 6.

covenant, Moses and Elias. But what is the relation of the disciples to this allegorical vision? Peter goes so far as to wish to build tabernacles for the common and permanent abode of all three; that is, he desires to see the transient and the permanent, the old and the new, the letter and the spirit, associated for all time,—"he knew not what he said; for they were sore afraid, and a cloud was overshadowing them."[1]   In this you have the allegorical illustration of the utterance of Paul, "their minds were hardened, for unto this very day the same veil lieth over the reading of the Old Testament, it not being revealed that it is done away in Christ." And just as the disciples were unable to understand the meaning of the transfiguration (resurrection), namely, that thereby Jesus became the Lord, who is spirit and freedom; so neither could they understand the true purpose of God in the case of the scriptural utterance regarding the sufferings of the Son of Man.[2]   And on that very

---

[1] Mark ix. 5 sq. ; comp. 2 Cor. iii. 14.

[2] Mark ix. 12, 32 ; comp. 2 Cor. iv. 4, v. 16, 17 ; Gal. vi. 12.

account they are then likewise unable to expel in Christ's name the evil spirits of Heathenism, and thereby betray the fact that, notwithstanding all their long intercourse with Jesus, they lack still (true) faith;[1] whilst, on the other hand, one who did not follow in the company of the disciples of Jesus, cast out demons in his name and worked miracles, and for that reason is acknowledged by Jesus as a disciple, whom the others ought not in their jealousy to hinder in his beneficent activity.[2] Thus the Pauline Evangelist makes Jesus himself the apologist of the greatly reviled Apostle Paul, who, though the last of the Apostles, had yet laboured more than all the rest, who, notwithstanding their intercourse with Jesus, of which they boasted to Paul's disadvantage, were censured by Jesus himself as a faithless generation with hardened hearts and blinded eyes. This was the Pauline reply, to the glorification of the Twelve in the Apocalypse, at the cost of the Apostle to the Heathen.

---

[1] Mark ix. 18, 19 ; comp. Gal. ii. 6, iii. 5.

[2] Mark ix. 38, 39 ; comp. 1 Cor. xii. 3, xv. 9, 10 ; 2 Cor. xii. 11, 12.

Jewish Christianity, thus attacked with weapons from the arsenal of Gospel tradition, made its reply in the "Gospel according to Matthew." In this Gospel, the earlier one of Mark has been combined with copious additional materials, consisting of discourses of Jesus, and taken from Galilean tradition; and the combination has been effected in such a way that the author, who occupies the same position as the writer of the Apocalypse, urges his dissent from both the Pauline freedom from the Law and the narrow particularism of the Jews. At the very beginning of the lengthy "Sermon on the Mount," to which is assigned such a prominent position as the programme of the labours of Jesus, the Evangelist inserts into the materials before him a few sentences which contain unmistakably an allusion to the Apostle Paul : "Whosoever therefore shall break one of these least commandments and shall teach men so, shall be called *the least* in the kingdom of heaven; but whosoever shall do and teach them, he shall be called great in the kingdom of heaven."[1]

---

[1] Matt. v. 19; comp. 1 Cor. xv. 9, ἐλάχιστος.

The humblest part is here assigned to Paul in the kingdom of heaven, with an evident intentional allusion to his own personal confession, because both in practice and teaching he broke the small things of the Law (the "letter"); a share in the kingdom of heaven is not altogether denied him (which would have been necessary in opposition to an ungodly antinomianism); but it is only equal rank and equal rights with the first Apostles, for which Paul had so often contended, that are absolutely refused him by the Jewish-Christian Evangelist. Peter, on the other hand, is represented expressly as "the first."[1] If Paul himself had based his full Apostleship on an immediate revelation from God, finding in this more than a sufficient compensation for his imperfect acquaintance with Christ after the flesh,[2] the Evangelist Matthew, on the contrary, makes this immediate revelation of God, which had not been communicated through "flesh and blood," the pre-eminent distinction of

---

[1] Matt. x. 2, πρῶτος, and v. 19, μέγας.

[2] Gal. i. 16, 17 ; 1 Cor. ix. 1 ; 2 Cor. x. 7.

Peter; and for the same reason he causes the "keys
of the kingdom of heaven" to be committed to him,
with authority to "bind and loose" (to legislate
as to things forbidden and permitted), and represents the "Church" of Christ as built for all time
upon the immovable rock of his authority;[1]—a
glorification of the "Pillar-Apostle," the historical
authenticity of which is disproved beyond doubt
both by the internal difficulties of the whole passage
and by its absence from the other Gospels. But
whilst the Apostle Paul himself is attacked in the
first Gospel and put below the first Apostles only in
a covert and indirect manner, Pauline antinomianism, on the other hand, is repudiated directly and
unconditionally as unchristian. In the highest
degree characteristic in this respect is the turn
which the Jewish-Christian Gospel has given to the
conclusion of the Sermon on the Mount, where Jesus
is made to say, "Many will say to me in that day,
Lord, Lord, have we not prophesied in thy name,
cast out devils and done many mighty works? And

---

[1] Matt. xvi. 17—19.

then will I profess unto them, I never knew you; depart from me, ye that work lawlessness!"[1] We hear in these words plainly the judgment of a legalistic Jewish Christian upon those Paulinists who call Jesus their Lord, are accustomed to speak of him in exalted language, and perform miracles also in his name, but who will, notwithstanding all that, not be acknowledged by the Messiah as his followers, for the reason that they work "lawlessness." It may be true that the Evangelist was thinking in this passage primarily of those ultra-Paulinists whose antinomianism had degenerated into heathenish libertinism; still he has not given the slightest indication of any marked difference between this extreme offshoot and the truly Pauline party, and therefore most likely did not himself make the distinction at all; on the contrary, he has evidently confounded Paulinism and libertinism, regarding them simply as both products of the same reprehensible principle of "lawlessness," differing from each

---

[1] Matt. vii. 21—23 (the peculiar form of expression must be observed, οἱ ἐργαζόμενοι τὴν ἀνομίαν).

other only in degree. We met with exactly the same thing in the Apocalypse; and this inability to distinguish between a moral and an immoral "lawlessness" is thoroughly characteristic of Jewish Christianity generally, and is most closely connected with the primary principles of the Religion of Law, according to which the positive Law is equally obligatory in all its parts, and the violation of any one commandment equally reprehensible with that of the rest. Though in daily life numerous restrictions of this principle had to be allowed, Jewish Christianity could not give up the principle itself without surrendering its own existence; for this reason a *modus vivendi*, and not a reconciliation on principle, was all that was ever possible between Paulinism and Jewish Christianity. This statement is confirmed by all the productions of this party in the first Christian age, not excepting those of a moderate tone, to which, it must be allowed, the Gospel of Matthew belongs.

For this Gospel is as far removed as the Apocalypse from a narrow Jewish particularism. It has transmitted, it is true, a few sayings, derived undoubtedly from the Palestinian sources used by the author, in which an extension of the mission of Jesus and his disciples beyond the national limits of Israel appears to be disavowed.[1] But side by side with this apparent limitation, we find in the woman of Canaan and the Heathen centurion models of Gentile faith presented with a view of shaming unbelieving Judaism;[2] in several parables the call of the Heathen in the room of the Jews, who had rejected the call which they had been the first to receive, is anticipated;[3] and, lastly, when Christ is parting from the disciples, the final command is put into his mouth,[4] "Go ye and make disciples of all nations, baptizing them and teaching them all things which I have commanded you." The action of the Apostles, which was the opposite of this injunction with regard to the Gentile mission, is proof that they did not remember having heard such a commission; this command must therefore have originated in the later period when our Evangelist wrote, and when Jewish Christians could no longer contest

---

[1] Matt. x. 5, 6, xv. 24, 26.

[2] Matt. viii. 10—12.

[3] Matt. xxi. 43, xxii. 6, 7.

[4] Matt. xxviii. 18, 19.

or ignore the actual successes of the Gentile mission,
and might feel it was more to their interest to let
the honour of those successes rest upon the original
Apostles as well as upon Paul, and upon them before
him. In what sense and under what conditions, however, the first Evangelist can sanction the mission
to the Heathen, he indicates by the further clause,
" teaching them all things which I have commanded
you ;" with regard to which we must remember that,
according to the first Evangelist, the " all things"
signify the validity of the whole Law, the smallest
letter of which, as we are told elsewhere (v. 18),
must not be broken. The same thing is intended
by that episode, peculiar to the first Evangelist, in
the parable of the royal Wedding-feast, according to
which one guest appears without a wedding garment. The explanation of this episode is supplied
in the passage of the Apocalypse, from which the
Evangelist without doubt took the figure : at the
Messianic marriage feast the Lamb's bride will be
arrayed in a pure, bright silk garment, which will
signify " the righteous acts of the saints."[1]   The

---

[1] Rev. xix. 8 ; Matt. xxii. 11 sq.

meaning of the parable in Matthew's form of it is, accordingly, that to the blessings of the Messianic kingdom all men will have admission, including the Heathen, but only under the condition that they show themselves worthy of this honour by keeping the Law (as a whole, without excepting the small and external elements of it, v. 18, 19). We see how far *this* universalism is still removed from that of the Apostle Paul.

While in the Gospel according to Matthew moderate Jewish Christianity found its expression and organ, in the Gospel according to *Luke*, which was written somewhat later, Paulinism once more made itself heard, though it is not, it must be admitted, the pure Paulinism of the Apostolic age, but the popularized irenical Paulinism of the second, post-apostolic generation, which was directed not so much against an exclusive and aggressive Jewish Christianity, as against unbelieving Judaism, whilst it was on good terms with moderate Jewish Christians. The third Evangelist was in sympathy with his own age of the nascent universal Church, and he has given an account of the rise of Christianity adapted to the practical necessities of the time. For this reason his Gospel was written, far more than its two predecessors, under the influence of idealistic considerations of a dogmatic and practical religious nature : the Pauline conception of Christ has been sketched in the brilliant colours of apocalyptic poetry, upon the basis of numerous and varied historical traditions.

The life of Jesus previous to his public ministry is told in this Gospel much more fully than in the Gospel of Matthew. The Pauline ideas, that it was "the Son of God according to the spirit of holiness," "the Second Man from heaven," who in the fulness of the times was "born of a woman, made under the Law that he might redeem us"[1]—how marvellously has the third Evangelist managed to give expression to them in the profound yet childlike language and imagery of religious poetry ! In fact, in the narratives and hymns of his story of the birth and childhood of Jesus, the sweetest blossoms of the religious poetry of all times were woven by

---

[1] Rom. i. 4 ; 1 Cor. xv. 47 ; Gal. iv. 4, 5.

Luke into the garland which he hung round the
picture of the earthly life of the celestial Son of
Man.   While Matthew made the preaching of
Jesus open with the Sermon on the Mount, the
programme of which lies in the utterance, "I am
not come to destroy but to fulfil the Law and the
Prophets," and its conclusion in the sentence of
rejection upon the "workers of lawlessness," Luke,[1]
on the contrary, puts in the foreground the sermon
in the synagogue at Nazareth as a model of the
labours of Jesus, and though he makes him speak
of the fulfilment of Scripture, it is not the fulfilment
of the Law but of the promise.   But these "words
of grace" which proceed from the mouth of Jesus
are not understood by his fellow-townsmen; and
when he proceeds to remind them of previous examples of the preference of Gentiles to Israelites, they
cast him out of the town in indignation and seek to
kill him—an anticipation of the subsequent course
of events when Israel was offended at the Pauline
gospel of grace, and was provoked to angry jealousy

---

[1] Luke iv. 16—30.

by the entrance of the Heathen into Messiah's kingdom before themselves. To the anti-Pauline sentence of Matthew against the "workers of lawlessness," Luke gives an anti-Judaic turn;[1] to the fellow-countrymen and contemporaries of Jesus who place reliance on the fact that they have eaten and drunk in his presence and he has taught in their streets, Jesus makes reply in this passage: "I know you not whence ye are; depart from me, ye doers of iniquity!" In the same way Luke has omitted the anti-Pauline episode of the guest without a wedding garment in the parable of the Marriage Feast, substituting for it a further detail to symbolize the universal Gentile mission.[2] Again, peculiar to Luke is a series of parables and narratives, which, whatever foundation they may have had in the traditions used by him, in any case in Luke's version of them, plainly give expression to the relation to Judaic Christianity of Paulinism in a later stage. To this series belong especially

---

[1] Luke xiii. 25 sq. ; comp. Gal. ii. 6 ; 2 Cor. v. 16.

[2] Luke xiv. 16—24.

the parables of the Pharisee and Publican and the Prodigal Son, in which the justification of the penitent sinner is contrasted with the proud self-righteousness of the Jews. Who does not recognize in the sulky displeasure of the elder son at the kindness of the father towards the returned younger son the jealousy of Heathen Christians felt by Judaism, with its boastful self-righteousness?[1] It corresponds completely, also, to the irenical manner in which Paul had spoken, Rom. xi., with regard to the permanent validity of the hopes of Israel, when the elder son's jealousy is censured by the father as without justification, while the privileges of his primogeniture are not called in question. The parables of the Good Samaritan and the Rich Man and Lazarus have primarily, it is true, a general moral significance, and were taken by the Evangelist from existing (probably Ebionite) sources; but in the first of these parables the preference of the semi-Heathen Samaritan to the representatives of official Judaism serves the cause of the Heathen

---

[1] Luke xv. 28—32 ; comp. Rom. ix. 30—x. 4.

Christian party of the Pauline Evangelist, and to
the latter parable he has annexed a closing application,[1] which—entirely foreign to the original meaning of the parable—amounts to an accusation against
unbelieving Judaism, because it cannot be brought
to repent either by Moses and the Prophets or by
the miracle of the resurrection (of Christ) from the
dead.

Decidedly Pauline, however, as the attitude of
the third Evangelist is towards Judaism, his judgment with regard to Jewish Christianity and its
leaders, the first Apostles, is, on the other hand,
no less moderate.   He takes a conciliatory position
in this respect between the first Evangelist, who
glorified the older Apostles exclusively at the cost
of Paul, and the second, who placed them throughout in the most unfavourable light—a position
characteristic of the conciliatory nature of later
irenical Paulinism.   The attitude of the third Evangelist in this respect is illustrated by the way in
which he narrates the story of Peter's confession:

---

[1] Luke xvi. 27—31.

on the one hand, he omits (with Mark) the glorification of Peter as the rock of the Church and the
possessor of the keys of the kingdom of heaven
(recorded by Matthew), but, on the other hand, he
represses also the severe censure of Peter on that
occasion which the two previous Evangelists report.
The account of the commission of the Seventy
Apostles in addition to the Twelve, again, is peculiar to the third Evangelist; as the latter number
suggests Israel as the destination of the mission of
the first Apostles, so the larger number indicates
a mission to the Gentiles; for in Jewish tradition
seventy is the number of the Heathen nations, a
belief to which the legend of the Seventy Trans-
lators of the Old Testament into Greek also points.
The instruction to the Seventy to eat whatever is
set before them, wherever they find a reception in
a city,[1] can be understood only on the implied
supposition that Heathen cities are intended; the
admonition to the missionaries not to scruple to
partake of food which would be unclean to Jews

---

[1] Luke x. 8; comp. 1 Cor. x. 27.

is not only in complete accordance with the Pauline principle, but it is connected verbally with the direction of Paul, "Eat whatever is set before you." If the Seventy are therefore the representatives of the Pauline mission to the Heathen, we can the more readily understand how the Evangelist was able to describe their success as much greater than that of the Twelve; he passed over the latter with only a hasty glance, but when the Seventy have returned and with rejoicing tell of their power over demons (Heathenism), he makes Jesus say, "I beheld Satan fall as lightning from heaven;" that is, he perceives in the result of the Pauline mission to the Gentiles the victory of Christ over the empire of Heathenism. But it is noteworthy that immediately afterwards he causes Jesus to turn to "the disciples especially," that is, to the Twelve, with the words, "Blessed are the eyes which see what ye see!"[1]   According to the view of this irenical Paulinist, which we have found Luke to be, the happiness of having seen Jesus with their

_____

[1] Luke x. 23.

eyes remains, after all, the incontestable advantage
of the first Apostles, which prophets and kings must
envy them. The third Evangelist accordingly, with
an impartiality which has got beyond the region of
sectarian strife, ungrudgingly accords to each of
the two primitive Christian parties its peculiar pre-
eminence and its special historical position.

But while that is true, at the same time he does
not leave us in doubt as to the side towards which
his own sympathies incline. This appears not only
in the fact that he has to extol, in accordance with
the actual facts, the greater success of the Apostleship to the Gentiles; but apart from its outward
results, Pauline Christianity, with its deeper inward
life of faith, commends itself to him as the "better
part," in comparison with the anxieties and troubles
of the piety of works cultivated by Jewish Christians. For this is obviously the meaning of the
beautiful story of the sisters Martha and Mary.
When the busy Martha complains with reference to
her sister as she sits at the feet of Jesus listening to
his words, "Lord, carest thou not that my sister
leaveth me to serve alone? Bid her therefore that

she also help !"[1]—we seem to hear a James complaining of the "vain man" who will not comprehend that faith without works is dead. And when Jesus thereupon takes the part of the accused sister with the beautiful utterance, " Martha, Martha, thou hast much care and trouble, but there is one thing needful ! Mary hath chosen the good part which shall not be taken from her !"—we discern therein the paraphrase of the Pauline declaration, " We reckon therefore that a man is justified by faith apart from the works of the Law ;" and, " It is no longer I that live, but Christ liveth in me; for the life which I now live in the flesh I live in the faith of the Son of God, who loved me !" To the same class belongs also the suggestive and charming narrative of the two disciples on the way to Emmaus,[2] which is peculiar to the Gospel of Luke. As these disciples were not of the number of the Twelve, we shall be justified in considering them to belong, according to the intention of the Evangelist, to the

---

[1] Luke x. 40, 41 ; comp. Rom. iii. 28 ; Gal. ii. 20.

[2] Luke xxiv. 13—33.

Seventy, that is, to be representatives of Pauline Gentile Christianity and of Paul himself. Just as Jesus
manifested himself as the Christ raised from the cross
to his glory to Paul on the road from Jerusalem to
Damascus, when he was pursuing his way in spiritual blindness, so on the road from Jerusalem to
Emmaus Jesus drew near to these disciples and they
knew him not, because their eyes were still holden
with sorrow at his death. But Jesus opened their
eyes by showing to them from the Scriptures how
necessary it was that Christ should suffer such things
that he might enter into his glory : when he thus
opened to them on the way the Scriptures, their
hearts burned with fear and hope. In like manner
the heart of Paul burned with the fire of his inward
doubts and conflicts, as on the way to Damascus he
pondered the words of Scripture, from the prophecies
of which the necessity of the sufferings of Christ
had been proved to him. When Jesus, as the
evening had come on, turned in-doors with the
disciples and took bread, gave thanks, broke it and
gave to them, their eyes were at last opened, and he
was known of them in the breaking of the bread of

the Supper. Thus the Pauline Christian recognizes Christ as the living Lord and quickening Spirit, not merely from the testimony of Scripture, but also from the immediate mystical and experimental evidence of the Lord's Supper, in which the broken bread and the consecrated cup are the mysterious agents of fellowship in the death and life of Christ.

When, finally, Luke's Gospel makes Jesus ascend visibly to heaven,[1] he once more illustrates in this closing tableau the leading thought of his entire historical narrative: it is not the life of the Son of David of the Jewish-Christian gospel which he seeks to present as the fulfilment of the promises to Israel; no, he that has been taken up into heaven is also the celestial Man who came from heaven, the Pauline Son of God according to the spirit of holiness, the Second Adam, in whom the purposes of God with mankind are to be realized, "that we might receive the adoption of sons."[2] This ideal conception of Christ the third Evangelist has, with incomparable skill, developed dramatically into a

---

[1] Luke xxiv. 51.   [2] Gal. iv. 5.

vivid historical picture, which, though it falls behind that of the two previous Gospels as regards strict historical reality, excels it in point of high ideal truth. This Evangelist might to a certain extent say with Paul,[1] "Though others have known Christ after the flesh, *we* no longer know him thus; for old things are passed away, all things have become new." In the light of the consciousness of the new Christian spirit of divine sonship, he beheld and delineated the life of the Lord. And did he not thereby succeed in presenting the real historical truth in one sense? We may say, certainly, that the immediate authority for his sketch of the life of Jesus was the Pauline idea of Christ; but then we must at the same time ask, whence did Paul derive that spirit of divine sonship which he saw personified in Jesus? Was not the ultimate source of this new conviction in reality the spirit of Jesus, that original religious consciousness of his own relation to God which constituted the essential element of the personality of Jesus? In this sense we may therefore say with

---

[1] 2 Cor. v. 16.

truth that the most idealistic of the Synoptic Gospels, which is the most closely related to the spiritual Gospel according to John, has delineated the inmost *nature* of the religious personality of Jesus more faithfully than the other two, particularly the Jewish-Christian Gospel according to Matthew, which conceived the person of Jesus with closer reference to his outward historical appearance. Inasmuch as the fourth Gospel goes a step further upon this course of an idealistic, dogmatic and didactic delineation of the life of Jesus, upon which Luke had previously entered, the conception of Christ presented by that Gospel likewise exhibits the influence of the impulses which in the first instance proceeded from Paul. Thus it was "the last of the Apostles" who accomplished "more than all the others" in this as well as other spheres: the depth of his insight into the personality and the inwardness of his love of Christ have found expression in both the tender and fragrant poetry of the third and the profound speculation of the fourth Gospel, supplying thus those elements from which the theology of the Christian Church has ever since constructed its idea of Christ.

LECTURE V.

PAULINISM AND GNOSTICISM.

LECTURE V.

PAULINISM AND GNOSTICISM.

A GNOSTIC element lay from the very first in the Pauline gospel of the revelation of God in Christ, a fruitful germ of theological gnosis or speculative theology. Paul felt, it is true, that he had been called to preach the gospel not in persuasive wisdom of words, but in demonstration of spirit and power, that the faith of his churches might not be based upon the wisdom of men, but upon the power of God.[1] But though this gospel was to the Jews a stumbling-block and to the Gentiles foolishness, it embodied nevertheless the wisdom of God, namely, the mystery of the divine counsels of grace, which had been hidden, but was now revealed by

---

[1] 1 Cor. i. 17, 21, ii. 4, 5.

the spirit that searcheth the deep things of God, and which we have received from God in order that we may know the things given to us by God.[1] Although the natural man is not capable of understanding spiritual things, the believer whose mind has been enlightened by the Spirit of God is able to enter into the divine purposes of salvation which have been made known in Christ's death and resurrection, can put them before men in an intelligible form, can demonstrate their intimate connection with the general revelation of God in history, and can show how they are based upon the divine oracles of the Old Testament. This was in reality, as we have seen, the substance of Pauline theology, with its logical unfolding and demonstration of the "word of the Cross;" it was the *gnosis* of the mystery of the crucified Son of God, as revealed by God in the Apostle's mind. And in the radiance of this light which shone upon him from the face of Christ, the meaning and importance of the divine revelation of the Old Testament had grown

---

[1] 1 Cor. i. 23, 24, ii. 6—12.

clear to him; the "veil of Moses" which concealed
the Old Testament from the Jews, so that they
were unable to get to the spirit beneath the letter,
was for the Apostle done away in Christ;[1] the spirit
hidden beneath the letter was revealed to him,
enabling him to find in the Law and the Prophets
everywhere simply the preparatory agencies, promises, and types of the fulfilment in Christianity.

The subject-matter of this "pneumatic" interpretation of the Old Testament, which regards the
letter as the vehicle of a deeper spiritual sense, was
in Paul's case determined by his own personal religious experience; but in its technical method it was
directly connected with the form of Jewish theology
which was then cultivated especially in Alexandria.
In this Alexandrine school, notwithstanding the
greatest respect for the letter of tradition, there was
really involved a new line of thought, which was as
far removed from positive Judaism as it was closely
related to the idealism of Greek philosophy. This
school of thought would never have had of itself the

---

[1] 2 Cor. iii. 14.

power to break through the limitations of Judaism and to found a universal monotheistic religion; it lacked the religious force requisite for such a purpose; but when associated with the Pauline gospel of Jesus Christ, Alexandrianism might become an exceedingly effective agent in the promotion of Christian universalism, as its mode of thought was more intelligible and obvious to the minds of Jews and Gentiles than the peculiar dialectics of Paul.

This combination of Pauline and Alexandrine gnosis, which becomes of such great importance in all future times, meets us first in the *Epistle to the Hebrews*, which was written in the reign of Domitian by a Paulinist, educated in the Alexandrine school, with the object of proving to Jewish Christians (probably of the Roman and other Italian churches), who had been shaken in their faith, the superiority of Christianity over Judaism. This object was not proposed with a view to putting down an aggressive Judaism zealous for the Law, such as might still continue to prevail in Palestine, but for the instruction and encouragement of an oppressed minority. The Jewish feelings

of this minority had previously been hurt by the
preponderating influence of Gentile Christianity,
and now it was further threatened and assailed with
persecution for the name of Christ. It had consequently begun to waver in its Christian confession,
and to look back to the religious services of the
Synagogue.[1] It was necessary to show to these
people that everything that Judaism had offered in
the shape of religious institutions and means of
grace was supplied still better by Christianity, and
indeed by it alone in a perfect manner and one fully
satisfying the heart. Consequently the relation of
Judaism and Christianity is not conceived in this
book as that of the Law in antithesis to the Gospel,
as is the case in Paul's writings, but as that of the
imperfect, typical and transient saving institution
to the perfect archetypal and eternal one.   Both
the Law and the Gospel, therefore, are classed as
saving institutions, the centre of which is formed
by the priesthood with its service in the sanctuary,
where the covenant of God with His people is

---

[1] Heb. x. 23—35, especially ver. 25, $\kappa\alpha\theta\grave{\omega}s$ $\check{\epsilon}\theta os$ $\tau\iota\sigma\acute{\iota}\nu$.

administered. Everything possessed by Judaism re-appears in Christianity—the priesthood, the sanctuary, sacrifices, a covenant, a holy people of God, promises, blessings, Sabbath rest. But Christianity possesses all these things in a much higher form than Judaism: there a changing sinful priesthood, but here one that remains and is sinless; there perpetually-repeated sacrifices efficacious for outward purification only, here once for all the self-sacrifice of the holy life of Christ, which has effected for ever a lasting salvation and a purification of the conscience; there once every year the entrance of the high-priest into the earthly sanctuary, here once for all access to the heavenly holy-of-holies opened for all by the high-priest Christ who is enthroned in heaven. The fundamental conception of Christianity presented in the Epistle to the Hebrews lies in this idea of the celestial sanctuary with its divine high-priesthood.

But in this idea diverse conceptions are combined. At the basis lies the conception of the Jewish temple service, which the author, however, does not appear to have known by personal

acquaintance, but only from the study of the Penta-
teuch. When he, therefore, speaks of this earthly
worship as the poor copy, or shadow, of a perfect
celestial original,[1] it is evident that he has before
his mind the Alexandrine conception of the higher
or ideal world (κόσμος νοητός), of which the visible
world is only an imperfect copy. And this " higher
world " of Alexandrine idealism is again immediately connected in his thought with the " future
world" of Jewish-Christian eschatology, just as in
the Apocalypse the kingdom of God at the consummation of all things is conceived as the descent
of the heavenly Jerusalem. But a peculiarity of
the Christian Alexandrian is the identification of
this transcendental world of speculative thought, or
apocalyptic intuition, with Christianity, whereby
the paradox is produced, that Christianity appears
to be something that does not as yet belong to the
present but only to the future world. The solution
of this paradox, however, is found in the simple fact,
that the future world is conceived as likewise the

---

[1] Heb. x. 1.

higher world, or local heaven, being in so far a present reality, with which Christians are placed by Christ, the celestial High-priest, in such communication that they are able to taste the powers of it, and have already received its first gifts.[1] The chasm between the world of sense and the world of ideas which the philosophies of Plato and Philo vainly sought to fill up, and the removal of which Judaism referred to the future, had in the thought of the Christian Alexandrian been already bridged over, at all events at one point, namely, in the mediatorial personality of Jesus Christ, who has come from and been exalted to heaven : in his mediation as High-priest the Church of the new covenant possesses the sure " anchor of hope," which has connected it with the immovable kingdom of eternal things, and is supplied with a pledge of the future fulfilment of all its desires.[2] The Christian assurance of salvation in the breast of the author of the Epistle to the Hebrews depends, therefore, as completely as Paul's, though its origin is

---

[1] Heb. vi. 4, 5.   [2] Heb. vi. 19.

different, on the person of Jesus Christ, on his
atoning death and his exaltation to heaven.

The Christology of the Epistle to the Hebrews
is not less, but rather more, copious than that of
Paul, inasmuch as, together with the transcendental ideal view of Christ's person, it justly
assigns to the historical side of the life of Jesus
its due prominence, thereby seeking, like the Gospel of John, to combine the two views of Christ
with regard to which Paul and the First Church
were divided, though, we must confess, the reconciliation is not very thorough. On the one hand,
Christ is a divine being, exalted far above men and
angels, an effulgence of the glory and impress of
the nature of God, through whom He made the
world, and, indeed, a being who himself upholds
all things ($\tau\grave{\alpha}$ $\pi\acute{\alpha}\nu\tau\alpha$) by the word of his power,—
predicates which are evidently based on the Alex-
andrine doctrine of Wisdom and the Logos.[1] But
this celestial Son of God did not merely take upon
himself the flesh and blood of God's children here

---

[1] Heb. i. 2, 3; comp. Wisdom of Sol. vii. 22 sq.

below, but during his life on earth shared also their weaknesses and temptations, only without sin, learnt obedience by suffering, and, as a reward for his trials, was crowned with glory and honour, and became a merciful High-priest, who is able, wherein he himself suffered and was tempted, to succour the tempted.[1] According to the Epistle to the Hebrews also, the death of Christ is the central point of the work of redemption; that death, however, is not, as in Paul's Christology, the execution of the curse of the Law upon the vicarious representative of mankind, but it is partly the probationary suffering by the obedient bearing of which Jesus earned for himself "perfection" in celestial glory and gave us an example of patience under suffering, and it is partly a purifying expiatory sacrifice which, as more efficacious than the sacrifices of the Old Testament, effects the removal from the conscience of the defiling guilt of sin and the consecration of the covenant of the new community, and thereby abolishes the ancient sacrifices.[2]

---

[1] Heb. ii. 14, 18, 19, v. 7 sq.

[2] Heb. ii. 9, 10, v. 9, ix. 14, x. 14 sq.

The emphasis, therefore, in this Epistle is not laid on the passive endurance of death in expiation of the Divine wrath, but on the presentation of the acceptable sacrifice of a holy life, that is, on the moral feeling and motives of the offerer; as this true spiritual sacrifice, Christ's death puts an end to the material sacrifices of the Old Testament ritual, and inaugurates the worship of God in spirit and truth. Thus the author of the Epistle to the Hebrews arrives at the same result as Paul; he did not, however, reach it through the Pharisaic theory of atonement, but through the idea, derived from the symbolism of the Old Testament ritual, of a moral act of sacrifice—a new point of view, which is also met with in the Gospel of John, and which was unquestionably more likely to be generally understood than the very peculiar, half-Jewish and half-mystic, theory of atonement taught by Paul.

The effect of the death and redemption of Christ is, according to the Epistle to the Hebrews, the opening of the celestial world of perfect fellowship with God in the case of those who in the true spirit of faith follow the Author of their faith. In this Epistle, faith regards Christ not so much as its object as its model;[1] it does not signify a mystical identification with the crucified and risen Christ, but the moral and religious state of mind which is directed, according to the example of Jesus, in confident hope to the invisible world, and authenticates itself by faithful obedience in action and suffering. As this devout habit of mind, faith is in itself already morally excellent conduct, or righteousness, which is not, therefore, according to this Epistle, received by the believer as a gift of God, but is simply acknowledged and attested by God as a moral quality already possessed.[2] The Pauline antithesis of faith and works, faith and law, is here lost in the simpler idea of a devout state of heart well pleasing to God. If this might be regarded as in certain respects an approximation to the Jewish-Christian form of thought, the Epistle to the Hebrews nevertheless rejects Judaic legalism

---

[1] Heb. xii. 2, xiii. 13.

[2] Heb. xi. 4, 5, 33, 39.

not less decidedly than Paul.[1] It does not, it is
true, justify its renunciation of Judaism by means
of the bold paradoxes of the Pauline theory of the
Law, but its allegorical use of the ritualistic laws
of the Old Testament is really nothing else than
another way of putting the genuine Pauline thought,
that Christianity is the only perfect religion, to
which Judaism, as an imperfect earlier stage of
truth, must give place. With this form of stating
the idea, moreover, the relative truth of Judaism
and the positive historical connection of Christianity
with the old covenant, receive more clearly their
due acknowledgment than in the negative dialectics
of Paul. On this account the theology of the Alexandrine Paulinism of the Epistle to the Hebrews
was the better adapted to act as a neutral medium
in the reconciliation of the differences existing in
primitive Christianity.

A step further in the same direction was taken
by the Epistle which bears the name of *Barnabas*,
and originated in the same quarter. It likewise

---

[1] Heb. vii. 12, x. 9, iii. 3—6, 12—15.

seeks by an allegorical and typical interpretation of
the Old Testament to show that Christianity is the
true fulfilment of Judaism. But it does this by
depriving the national and legal form of Judaism of
even any relative importance, and simply condemn-
ing it as a demoniacal perversion of the truth.[1]
According to the view of Barnabas, the Lawgiver
never commanded the circumcision of the body,
but only of the heart and ears, of which the
prophets had previously spoken ; but the Jews,
deceived by a wicked angel, misunderstood the
Divine will and introduced physical circumcision,
which cannot, after all, be the true sign of the
covenant, inasmuch as it was practised likewise by
the Syrians, Arabians and Egyptians. The laws
regarding food, too, had originally simply the force
of moral allegories; the prohibition of the eating
of pork, for instance, signifying merely a general
warning against luxurious living, and the per-
mission of the ruminants, an allegorical admonition
to righteousness of life and devout rumination upon

---

[1] Barn. ii. iii. ix. x. xv. xvi.

the word of God; it was only the carnal mind of
the Jews that understood all these directions lite-
rally as referring to material food. The ordinance
of the Sabbath likewise was intended only to point
to the commencement of the new world at the
parousia of Christ, and found therefore its true
fulfilment in the Christian Sunday, as the day of
Christ's resurrection. The Jewish reverence for
the Temple particularly appears to Barnabas to
be a most unhappy Heathenish feeling, which God
himself condemned by the destruction of the edifice,
with the view of showing that the true Temple of
God is the heart of the saints, or believers. In like
manner God long ago declared by the Prophets that
He desires no other sacrifices than the offering of
the heart, and that the one fast acceptable to Him
is to shun evil and to do good (Isaiah lviii. 6 sq.).
By misinterpreting all these injunctions and observ-
ing them in an outward, carnal sense, instead of
understanding them in the true ethical sense which
God as well as Moses and the Prophets intended, the
Jewish nation, according to Barnabas, simply demon-
strated that it was not at all the people of God's

covenant which it claimed to be. This conclusion was confirmed also by the entire course of Israel's history, which, from the idolatry at Sinai to the crucifixion of Jesus, in which the nation filled up the measure of its sins, was one continuous demonstration of its reprobation.

This unqualified anti-Judaism undoubtedly grew up upon Pauline soil, but it has outgrown the feeling of Paul, who had, Rom. xi., earnestly censured and refuted a hard condemnation of Israel of this kind. It is, however, clear that it was only a short step from such a hyper-Pauline anti-Judaism as this to the Gnostic dualism of Marcion, who at last completely severed the historical connection between Christianity and Judaism. If the "gnosis" which the Epistle of Barnabas seeks to add to faith as a higher attainment[1] is not as yet strict Gnosticism in the heretical sense, inasmuch as it is not yet occupied with the transcendental world, but with the allegorical treatment of the history of reli-

---

[1] Barn. i. 5, ἵνα μετὰ τῆς πίστεως ὑμῶν τελείαν ἔχητε τὴν γνῶσιν.

gion, it represents, nevertheless, the transition from Christian Alexandrianism to heretical Gnosticism. But before we trace the further development of the hyper-Pauline gnosis, we must cast a glance at that form of it, acknowledged by the Church, which arose within orthodox Paulinism, under the influence of Alexandrianism, at the beginning of the second century, and has been preserved in the Epistles to the Colossians and Ephesians.

The design of the *Epistle to the Colossians*, which is a product of the Pauline school, is to oppose heretical teachers, who, though Judaizers, are of an entirely different class from those with whom the earlier Pauline Epistles contend. They appear to have been Christian Essenes, who sought to introduce their speculations with regard to the higher spirit-world, and the spiritualistic asceticism connected therewith, into Christianity, and in attention to this supposed higher truth and sanctity lost from under their feet the foundation of historical faith in Christ and of healthy moral church life. The Paulinism of the Church opposed to this false gnosis, which reminds us of Cerinthus, the true gnosis, to its phantastic

notions of the angels its own speculative Christology, to its Ebionite asceticism its own ideal
Christian morality. As the Colossian heretics had
put Christ on a level with the angels, or had even
made him subordinate to them, our orthodox
Paulinist teaches the exaltation of Christ beyond
all spiritual "powers" in language which reminds
us not merely of the earlier Pauline Christology,
but also of the Logos doctrine of Philo. Christ is,
according to our author, the centre of the universe;
all things were created not merely "through" him
but also "unto" him, and have in him their permanent consistence; all the fulness of the Godhead
dwelt in him bodily;[1] the incarnation of Christ,
accordingly, is no longer conceived (as in Paul's
Christology) as consisting in the laying aside of
celestial glory, but simply in the veiling of it in a
mortal body. To this cosmic position of Christ the
significance of his work of salvation fully corresponds: the atoning effect of the death of Christ is
no longer limited to the reconciliation of mankind

---

[1] Col. i. 15—19, ii. 9.

with God, but embraces the entire world of spiritual existences, the angelic powers of the invisible world being included in the pacification effected by Christ; Christ is therefore not only the centre of the creation, but also the atoning mediator of peace throughout the entire terrestrial and celestial universe.[1] He is likewise represented as the victorious vanquisher of the hostile spiritual powers, which, as possessors of "the document against us" (the Law), held the world captive, as it were, in their grasp.[2] The Pauline idea that Christ delivered us from the curse of the Law by vicariously bearing it himself, acquires therefore in the thought of the Gnostic Paulinist a reference to the dominion of the empire of demons, whose terrible power over the sinful world was overcome and destroyed by the death of Christ,—a conception which reminds us of the subsequent mythological notion of the conflict of Christ and the Devil. For the very reason that in Christ the powers of the universe have been vanquished or reconciled, the Christian ought no longer to

---

[1] Col. i. 20.   [2] Col. ii. 14, 15.

remain subject to them by the worship of angels
and a self-willed and scrupulous asceticism, but must
appropriate more and more completely the treasures
of wisdom and knowledge hidden in Christ, must
increase in the knowledge of God and walk worthy
of the Lord, bringing forth fruit in every good
work.[1]   The orthodox Paulinist, it is true, also
lays great stress on the place of knowledge in
Christianity, but in contradistinction to false Gnosticism he requires adherence to Christ as the Head
and to the fellowship of the Christian Church.

The practical turn thus given to the Pauline
gnosis was subsequently carried out further in a
fresh manner in the *Epistle to the Ephesians*, which
coincides completely with the Gospel of John in
theological tendency.   The affinity of this Epistle
with that to the Colossians has always been observed,
but the difference—by no means inconsiderable—
in the object and tone of the two has been usually
overlooked.   In the Ephesians there is not a trace
of the heresies combated in the Colossians; as far

---

[1] Col. ii. 12, 13, 9 sq., iii. 10.

as the former is polemical at all, its conflict is not
with Ebionite Jewish Christians but hyper-Pauline
Gentile Christians, not with a scrupulous asceticism
but a frivolous libertinism, not with Jewish particularism but Heathen, anti-Jewish arrogance and
want of brotherly love. The object of the Epistle
to the Ephesians was to restore unity between these
two parties, which still continued to divide the
Christian Church. It is just this which the author
regards as the subject-matter of the Gospel revelation, the purpose of the mission and the death of
Christ. The speculative teaching of the Epistle to
the Colossians regarding the reconciliation of the
celestial and terrestrial universe by Christ's death,
receives in our Epistle the ethical application, that
Heathen and Jews have been united by the death
of Christ into one body—the Church—by the
removal of the wall of partition in the Law.[1] The
essential object of the death of Christ, according to
this Epistle, is therefore no longer (as in Paul's
writings) redemption from the curse of the Law,

---

[1] Eph. ii. 14 sq.

but the foundation of the universal Church by the
harmonizing of all differences. The Christological
speculation of Colossians, that "the fulness of the
Godhead" dwelt bodily in Christ, comes in Ephesians to signify that the Church, as the body of
Christ, is "his fulness," that is, the complete realization of his divine nature in human form.[1] The
great emphasis which our Epistle puts on the continuous operation of the Holy Spirit as the source
of revelation in the Church, is connected with this
idea; the Spirit not only revealed Christian truth
through the Apostles, but still continues to reveal
it through the Christian prophets, whose inspired
glance penetrates the depths of divine wisdom.[2]
The Christian revelation is, accordingly, not an
accomplished fact of the past, but the continuous
and progressive development, in extent and depth,
of Christian knowledge in the Church—a thought
by which the Epistle is brought into direct rela-

---

[1] Eph. i. 23, iv. 13.

[2] Eph. i. 17, iii. 5, iv. 11 (*Christian* prophets, as the successors
of the Apostles, and not those of the Old Testament, are intended
here).

tions with the Gospel of John and with Montanism.[1]
When, finally, the call of the Gentiles into the
kingdom of Christ is described, Eph. iii. 5, as the
subject of a revelation which "the holy Apostles
and Prophets" had as a body received, we have
therein a plain indication of the irenical feeling of
the later Paulinism, which has forgotten or wishes
to ignore the differences of the Apostolic age. The
Epistle to the Ephesians is accordingly a significant
monument of the desire of union characteristic of
the Paulinism of the second century, from which
we learn that the reconciliation of the various parties
was then felt on the part of the Paulinists to be an
urgent necessity.

The last act of the hundred years' conflict between
Gentile and Jewish Christians was performed in
the Roman Church in the middle of the second
century. But this final act differed essentially
from previous ones in that it was no longer parties

---

[1] Eph. i. 17 sq., iv. 13 sq. ; comp. John xvi. 12 sq., and
Tertull. *De Virgin. Veland.* i.

within the Church which were at war with each
other, but the heretical extremes, on the right and
the left, whilst the Church in opposition to them
maintained a neutral intermediate position, and
strengthened its unity in the midst of this very
conflict with overstrained and extravagant tendencies. The older Gnostic systems, with their turbid
mixture of Hellenistic philosophy and Oriental
mythology, could not make any way in sober and
practical Rome. On the other hand, the gifted
Gnostic *Marcion* of Sinope found there suitable
soil for his violently anti-Judaistic hyper-Paulinism. When he came to Rome, in the reign of
Antoninus Pius and during the episcopacy of Pius
(142 A.D.), he sought at first to attach himself to
the Catholic Church, but soon betrayed his heretical doubts and inclinations by the captious exegetical questions which he proposed to the teachers.
The Syrian Gnostic *Cerdon*, who was at that time
teaching in the capital, exercised a decisive influence
upon him. Cerdon had been led by the antipathy
to matter which was traditional in Oriental speculation, to place the Creator of the material world

as an imperfect God in contrast with the God and
Father of Jesus.[1] The wavering position of this
teacher towards church fellowship did not deter
his bolder disciple Marcion from deducing the
consequences of that metaphysical dualism in relation to the religious consciousness, in such a way
as to put Christianity in absolute and exclusive
opposition to every pre-Christian, and especially to
the Jewish, religion. The peculiar importance and
the profound influence of Marcion on the Church
are based upon this very fact, that, leaving out of
view its transcendental speculations and cosmo-
logical mythologies, he applied Gnosticism directly
to practical religious questions; and to this too was
owing the fierce opposition which he, more than
any other heretic of the first centuries, met with
from the orthodox Fathers.

The starting-point and hinge of Marcion's system
are nothing else than Paulinism exaggerated to
the utmost. Paul had placed Christianity as the

---

[1] Tertull. *Adv. Marc.* i. 2 ; Iren. *Adv. Hær.* i. 27, 1, iii. 4, 3 ;
Hipp. *Philosophumena*, vii. 37, x. 19.

"newness of the spirit" in contrast with Judaism
as the system of the letter which killeth; and he
had denominated the ritual of the Law of Moses
the worship of the weak and beggarly elements of
the world, from which the Christian has been delivered by faith in the Son of God.   The authors of
the Epistles to the Hebrews and the Colossians had
acknowledged in the Jewish ritual types of higher
things, but still only an unsubstantial and powerless
prefiguration of the truth revealed in Christianity.
The strictly Pauline and otherwise soundly orthodox author of the Epistle of Barnabas had gone
further, and pronounced legalistic Judaism, with
its literal interpretation of the ceremonial Law, a
perversion of the real intention of God, having its
origin in demoniacal infatuation.   We have but to
advance another step and we find ourselves on the
standpoint of Marcion, who pronounces the God
of Judaism another and less perfect being than the
God of Christianity.   The same wide difference
which exists between the Law and the Gospel as
religious principles, and between the material world,
with which the commands and promises of the Law

are concerned, and the celestial world of evangelical promise, must, according to Marcion, likewise
exist between the authors of the two religions.[1]
The Jewish God, or the "Demiurgus," as Marcion
denominated him after the customary Gnostic ter-
minology, is as legislator and judge only righteous,
severe and cruel, not good, kind and merciful, like
the God of the Gospel. Marcion sought to establish
this exegetically and dogmatically, by collecting all
the accounts of the Old Testament in which human
feeling is ascribed to God, and also by referring
to contradictions between the commands of God
and His way of acting on various occasions; the
story of the Fall especially appeared to him to
be inconsistent with the perfection of the Divine
Being,—with His goodness, or truth, or power.[2]
He was as little able to find a revelation of the
true God in the Heathen religion of nature as in
the Jewish religion of law; the material world of
nature appeared to the spiritualistic Gnostic much

---

[1] Tertull. *Adv. Marc.* i. 19.

[2] Ibid. ii. 5, 11, 12, 20, *et al.*

too mean and impure to be possibly the work of
the perfect and true God. The true God had therefore always remained unknown to the ancient world;
He was first revealed by Christianity. And the
revelation of the true God in Christianity was
conceived by Marcion as given without the inter-
position of any historical medium, as an absolute
miracle. The Pauline Christ was by nature the
spiritual Man from heaven, but as regards the flesh
he was at the same time connected with terrestrial humanity, especially with the fathers of Israel.
This connection Marcion endeavoured at all costs
to remove: his Christ must have nothing to do with
either a Jewish extraction or a natural physical life.
For this reason he denied his possession of a true
human body and his human birth; Christ, he taught,[1]
descended to the earth directly from heaven as
pure spirit in a merely illusive body ("phantasma")
and appeared forthwith in the synagogue at Caper-
naum. The other Gnostics had taught Docetism,
in a form more or less similar to this, but in their

---

[1] Tertull. *Adv. Marc.* i. 19, iii. 11, iv. 7.

case it had its basis in a metaphysical theory of the
relation of spirit to matter; in Marcion's system,
on the other hand, the real source of it was not so
much a metaphysical theory as the religious postulate, that Christianity must be conceived as something absolutely new, a sudden miracle, without any
natural and historical connection with the earlier
human race—the exaggeration of the Pauline idea,
that in Christ there is neither Jew nor Greek, but
a new creature. The Epistle of Barnabas had also
given a direct precedent for this postulate, as it
expressly recognized in Christ the Son of God only,
and not also the Son of Man.[1] We have a specially
clear illustration of the great predominance in Marcion's Docetism of the religious over the speculative aim, in the surprising want of consistency
(justly censured by Tertullian)[2] which he displays
in decidedly maintaining the truth of the passion
and death of Christ, though he denied his birth
and his possession of a real human body. The

---

[1] Barn. xii. 10 (with an appeal to Ps. cx. 1 ; comp. Matt.
xxii. 42, 43).

[2] Tertull. *Adv. Marc.* iii. 8.

reason of this inconsistency is clear: by a true human birth Christ would have been brought into connection with the realm of the Demiurgus, while the death which he suffered in consequence of the enmity of the Demiurgus was the manifestation of the absolute opposition between the two principles, and thereby prepared for the overthrow of the realm of the ruler of this world; for by committing the mistake of procuring the crucifixion of the Holy One, the Demiurgus forfeited his claim to rule the world. It is easy to discern in this a mythological expansion of the Pauline idea of Christ having redeemed us from the curse of the Law by becoming a curse for us, or of our having died to the Law through the Law. As Paul, finally, had deduced from his gnosis of the crucifixion of Christ the practical consequence that we ought to regard ourselves as dead to sin and to crucify the flesh with its lusts, so Marcion drew similar inferences from his dogmatic Christology, in this case again so exaggerating the Pauline idealism as to make of it an inflexibly rigorous asceticism, to which everything natural appeared reprehensible. The married state especially was looked upon by Marcion and his school with great disfavour, as a condition belonging to the ungodly realm of the Demiurgus, from which the true Christian, as a member of the immaterial realm of the good God, must abstain;[1] the contraction of marriage was prohibited to the members of the sect, and from those already married the strictest abstinence was required. Beyond doubt this extravagant asceticism was, not less than his dogmatic vagaries, a reason for the decided condemnation of Marcion by the entire Catholic Church, including the moderate Paulinists particularly, whose special interest it was to decline any compromising fellowship with the hyper-Paulinists.

In this attitude of the Church we have an illustration of what so frequently happens in history— by the undue emphasis of a principle a reaction is provoked which undervalues and suppresses the relative truth of the position oppugned. Because Marcion exaggerated the Pauline antithesis of the

---

[1] Tertull. *Adv. Marc.* i. 29, iv. 34.

Law and the Gospel, the Church brought the two into such close proximity that the Gospel was made for it into a new Law. Because Marcion acknowledged Paul alone as the true Apostle of Christ—he accepted only ten Pauline Epistles and a mutilated Gospel of Luke as genuine Scriptures, and maintained that the Jewish Christians had adulterated the truth of the Gospel—the Church in turn would know nothing at all of the opposition between the first Apostles, and put Peter on an equality with Paul, or, indeed, before him. In proportion as the Gnostic excrescences of antinomian Paulinism threatened the existence of the Christian Church, the reputation of Peter rose in general estimation, his name being regarded as the watchword of historical conservatism and ecclesiastical authority, such as was required by the age, and which the Roman Church especially felt called upon to establish.

To this orthodox reaction against the hyper-Paulinism of Marcion, the religious party fiction (*Tendenzroman*) which appeared in the middle of the second century under the name of "Homilies and Recognitions of *Clement*," owed its wide circulation and popu-

larity in the Roman Church. The story of this fiction
is extremely meagre, and serves merely as the framework for a series of public debates between Peter
and Simon Magus. The part played by this legend-
ary magician and arch-heretic represents generally
the heresy of Marcion, but occasionally the Gentile
Apostle Paul also, who is accordingly regarded by
the author as the intellectual originator of that
heresy. In the letter of Peter to James, prefixed
to the work, the Judaic author gives expression to
his antipathy to Paul by making Peter complain
that some of the Gentiles have adopted the anti-
legal and foolish doctrine of the *inimicus homo* and
interpret his (Peter's) words as if he had been
equally hostile to the Law, but did not venture to
declare his opposition as openly—an evident allusion
to the charge of hypocrisy made against Peter by
Paul in Antioch. The old point of contention with
regard to the Apostolic dignity of Paul, for which
the Apostle himself had had to fight so many
battles, was also now raised afresh.[1] Simon Magus

---

[1] Hom. xvii. 13—19.

appeals to his visions, maintaining that by them he has obtained a better knowledge than Peter of the true nature of Jesus. To this Peter replies that visions and dreams cannot yield certain knowledge, as it can never be known whether some lying spirit or wicked demon may not be at the bottom of them. Indeed, this is the more probable, as the immaterial form of God, or of His Son, could not be really seen by mortals on account of its transcendent light. Hence, from the fact that a man has had visions or dreams, it cannot by any means be inferred with certainty that he is a pious man. On the contrary, the truth is revealed to the pious by virtue of a pure inborn sense of it; it is imparted to the godly by insight and not by dreams. In the heart put by God within us dwells the germ of all truth, and by God's hand it is veiled or revealed. When Simon (Paul) maintains that a man may be instructed by visions, so as to become a teacher, it is asked in reply, Why, then, did the Lord spend a whole year in intercourse with men who were awake? And how can we believe that the Lord has appeared to him, since he really holds

opinions opposed to the teaching of the Lord?
"But if thou hast really been made by him an
Apostle by virtue of the vision and instruction of a
single hour, declare his words, expound his doctrine,
love his Apostles, and do not contend with me
who have had intercourse with the Lord! Thou
hast as an antagonist withstood me, who am the
immovable rock and the foundation of the Church.
If thou wert not an enemy, thou wouldst not have
scorned me and reviled my preaching, in order
that I may not be believed when I speak the things
which I have heard from the Lord himself. Or if
thou pronouncest me 'condemned' (Gal. ii. 12),
thou layest a charge against God, who revealed
Christ to me, and thou censurest Him who called
me blessed on account of this revelation (Matt.
xvi. 18). But if thou art determined really to
labour with us for the truth, learn from us first
those things which we have learnt from the Lord,
and having thus become a disciple of the truth, be
our fellow-labourer."—Thus deep was the ill feeling
on account of the contention in Antioch in Jewish-
Christian circles as late as the middle of the second

century! Thus tenaciously was the opposition to the Apostolic office of Paul and the doubt as to his Apostolic call still maintained!

The opposition of pseudo-Clement is directed not less decidedly against the dogmatic positions of the Pauline preaching. In his view, so far is Christianity from being a new covenant and a new creation, that it is, on the contrary, nothing else than purified and reformed Judaism. The doctrine of Moses and Jesus, he says, is one and the same, and God therefore accepts every man who believes on either of them and observes the commands of either in practice. And whoever is counted worthy to recognize both as preachers of the same doctrine, and comes to perceive that old things have in course of time become new and new things old, must be counted as a rich man in God.[1] While Marcion, going beyond the Pauline idea, put Judaism and Christianity in opposition to each other as the religion of the Law and the religion of the Gospel, or of the just and of the good God, according

---

[1] Hom. viii. 5—7.

to pseudo-Clement Judaism is already the true
religion, as it acknowledges the one Father and
Creator of the universe, who is not less good than
just—just as the Judge rewarding our deeds, good
as forgiving the sins of the penitent. Wherein
Christianity surpasses Judaism is simply that it
removed the subsequent additions to the primitive
divine revelation and made the latter known again in
its first purity. Among these adulterating accretions
pseudo-Clement reckons the whole of the ceremonial
portion of the Mosaic Law, together with its national
restriction to the Jews; further, all those expres-
sions with regard to God's attributes or actions
which do not accord with a spiritual or moral conception of Deity; finally, those narratives of the
Old Testament in which things morally offensive
are ascribed to righteous and favoured men of God.
Such portions of the Jewish tradition and the Old
Testament did not come from the true revelation,
but from false prophecy, which is, like Heathenism,
of demoniacal origin. It is to them the saying of
Jesus refers, " Every plant which my heavenly
Father hath not planted shall be rooted up." The

proof that Jesus did not regard such things as belonging to the true Law, which must remain until heaven and earth pass away, is found by Clement in the simple fact, that the Jewish sacrifices, monarchy and prophets, have actually passed away, while the heavens and earth still remain.[1]

We see that, with all his repudiation of the dualism of Marcion, pseudo-Clement nevertheless applies to historical Judaism a degree of criticism which in point of boldness is scarcely second to the Marcionite anti-Judaism. In order to prove the unity of Christianity and Judaism, the Gospel and the Law, he distinguishes in Judaism itself between the ideal essence of eternal truth and the positive, nationally limited form; and the first he accepts as revealed, whilst he ascribes to the second a demoniacal origin, and puts it on a level with Heathenism. The Pauline author of the Epistle of Barnabas had previously made just the same distinction. Thus the Paulinist and the anti-Paulinist joined hands in that intermediate position of the universal Church,

---

[1] Hom. iii. 52.

where everything of a nationally limited character
that did not harmonize with the universalism of the
Church was removed from Judaism, while whatever
appeared to the Church as likely to support her
authority in faith and practice was retained. Whatever in Paulinism was of directly practical importance for the nascent Church—its universalism and
its abrogation of the Jewish ceremonial Law—
advanced Jewish Christianity had by this time
appropriated; but it made these concessions to the
force of accomplished facts only with a view of the
more decisively maintaining and forcing upon the
Church, now becoming universal, its principle of
righteousness by works, and a legal ecclesiastical
constitution in opposition to the Pauline principle
of faith and the emancipating spirit.

In other respects we must acknowledge that the
Jewish-Christian gnosis of pseudo-Clement com-
pares advantageously with the speculative and
ascetic bent of Marcion in point of wise moderation
and large-hearted tolerance. While, according to
Marcion, Christ descended direct from heaven as an
absolutely miraculous being, without any historical

relation to the human race, pseudo-Clement saw in
him the last and highest revelation of the same
divine prophetic spirit as had previously appeared
in Adam, the Patriarchs and Moses, which is not
essentially different from the eternal spirit of God
implanted in all men. Since Adam had already
the holy spirit of Christ, as pseudo-Clement repeatedly asserts,[1] Christ is not an absolutely new and
supernatural phenomenon, but simply the most
perfect manifestation of the ideal man, only rela-
tively different from previous and less perfect mani-
festations of the one divine spirit of humanity.
It is impossible not to recognize in this theory a
certain affinity to the Pauline doctrine of Christ as
the second Adam; the Christology of Paul may
therefore claim to be the common root of the two
schools of Gnosticism: in Marcion's system it was
further developed in the direction of an abstract
pneumatological Docetism, while in that of pseudo-
Clement it takes the form of a natural and historical
Ebionitism. If, according to Marcion, the entire

---

[1] Hom. iii. 20, xviii. 14.

pre-Christian race, both Jews and Gentiles, was
under the dominion of the imperfect Demiurgus
and without a knowledge of the true God, according
to pseudo-Clement the knowledge of the truth is
implanted in all men's hearts, and is revealed more
or less clearly to them by God in proportion to
their worthiness.[1] As man bears in his nature the
image of his Creator, the good God, he is able and
ought to become like God by purity of mind and the
performance of what is good, and especially ought
he to revere the image of God in his fellow-men by
a practical exhibition of his love. Grateful love of
God, which evinces itself in the love of those who
bear God's image, is the innate and inalienable
dignity of man.[2] On that account the Heathen is
able to do what is truly good, and to make himself
by his virtue worthy of the higher revelation of
Christ, as is illustrated in the instance of Clement
himself and his chaste mother. If, finally, Marcion,
in consequence of his dualistic view of the material
world, had taught a monkishly ascetic form of

---

[1] Hom. xvii. 18.   [2] Hom. xi. 4, 8, 27.

morals, and had even repudiated marriage as dis-
pleasing to God, the monotheist pseudo-Clement
recognizes in the material world and in natural life
a divine creation, intended for the service of man
and the furtherance of his moral purposes; according to his conviction, marriage is so far from being
reprehensible that he directs the bishops to exhort
young people to marry at the proper time; and with
fine moral feeling he sketches the ideal of Christian
wedlock—how, when consecrated by piety, it has
its firm basis in mutual esteem and love, and by
self-discipline and decorum avoids all perils and
seductions.[1]

In fact, this ideal of the moral life exhibits that
sober wisdom which does not soar in visionary
enthusiasm above the actual life of human society,
but seeks to ennoble it by the sacred motives of
religion, and thereby helps to qualify the Church
to fulfil its practical work of educating the world.
When we consider further the great stress put upon
the authority of the Church, which anticipated the

---

[1] Hom. xiii. 18, xi. 23.

necessities of the time and was absolutely required for the development of Christianity in the midst of enemies without and strifes within, we can understand why the Homilies of the anti-Pauline pseudo-Clement should find favour in the Roman Church, where, nevertheless, the memory of Paul had never ceased to be held in high honour, and that they should be used to increase the influence of Peter as the representative of historical authority.

LECTURE VI.

PAULINISM AND THE CHURCH.

PAULINISM AND THE CHURCH.

In view of the growing dangers from without and within, the most urgent task put before the Christian Church of the first half of the second century was to reconcile in complete ecclesiastical unity Jewish and Gentile Christians, and at the same time to give stable organization to the Church by the development of its offices as representative of ecclesiastical tradition and authority. We have seen that Jewish Christianity first anticipated this want of the time, by putting decisively into force its spirit of legal discipline, represented in the person of Peter, though it suffered the national form of its legalism to drop. But neither had Paulinism been able to escape the tendency of the age; it likewise made concessions, though not so much to the Jewish-Christian party as to the rising Catholic Church. In some respects the larger sacrifice even was on its part: for though it retained the form of Pauline doctrine, it exchanged the Pauline spirit of evangelical freedom and individual charismatic enlightenment for the "new Law" of ecclesiastical custom and authority. This transformation of Paulinism into Catholicism may be traced with growing distinctness in the Epistle of Clement of Rome to the Corinthians, in the Pastoral Epistles to Timothy and Titus, and finally in the so-called Ignatian Epistles.

The *Epistle of Clement of Rome to the Corinthians*, written at the end of the first century, is in several respects a document of the greatest importance in relation to the first period of ecclesiastical history. As a letter from the Church at Rome to that at Corinth, the design of which is the adjustment of certain disputes and disorders in the latter community, the document supplies the first trace of a supremacy of the Roman Church in Christendom. And it enables us to surmise the grounds of this supremacy. They are not derived simply from the consecration of this Church by the martyrdom of the two foremost Apostles, which is mentioned for the first time in this Epistle (unless we have a still earlier trace of it in Rev. xviii. 20); they are to be found much more in the amalgamation of Paulinism and Petrinism in an intermediate neutral union, in the subordination of dogmatic, to practical ecclesiastical interests, and in the enforcement of the principle of authority, order and subordination, in contradistinction to the Pauline principle of the possession of the spirit and the free exercise of individual faith. The dogmatic form of Paulinism is preserved, it is true; as far as dogma is at all alluded to, the modes of expression used in the Epistles to the Romans and the Hebrews are retained (with which two authorities this of Clement forms the third, in proof of the predominant Heathen-Christian and Pauline character of the first Roman Church). Redemption through the blood of Christ is frequently spoken of,[1] Christ having given his

---

[1] Clem. Ep. I. ad Cor. xlix. xxi. xii. vii.

flesh for our flesh and his soul for our soul (as a substitutionary expiation), from love to us and according to the will of God; we must steadily look at the blood of Christ, and perceive how precious it is to God, since as shed for our salvation it procured the grace of repentance for the whole world (the possibility of being reconciled to God by grace on the condition of penitent faith, comp. Rom. iii. 25, ἱλαστήριον διὰ τῆς πίστεως). Clement accepts very emphatically the cardinal Pauline doctrine of justification by faith: "We are not justified by ourselves, nor by our own wisdom, or intelligence, or godliness, or by the works which we did in holiness of heart, but by faith, by which God justified all the pious from the beginning."[1]   But inasmuch as Clement conceives of faith according to the wider view of it met with in the Epistle to the Hebrews, as the devout condition of confidence in and obedience to God, it no longer forms the antithesis to works, but is itself moral action, which *effects* righteousness (is not merely recipient

---

[1] Ep. I. ad. Cor. xxxii.

of it, as in Paul's view). Consequently Clement
can also speak, like James, of being "justified by
works and not by words," and of "forgiveness of
sins by love, which in concord fulfils the precepts
of God."[1] The emphasis is no longer placed on
religious mysticism, but on moral practice, and the
regulative principle of the latter is found, not in
the inward law of the holy Spirit, but in the
social customs and constitution of the Church,
which, again, obtains its model and its authority
from the legal regulations of the theocratic nation
of the Old Testament. It is true, Paul had confined
the freedom of Christians within the limits of love,
which fulfils the law of Christ in the service of the
brethren; but since love has within itself its own
normal principle, Paul recognized in the "law of
Christ" a "*law of the spirit*" which brings liberty,
not a law of the letter which enslaves. But this
truly Pauline idealism, which discovers the gospel
of the freedom of God's children in the depths of
the soul, was beyond the reach of the Roman with

---

[1] Ep. I. ad Cor. xxx. 1.

his practical and political habit of thought; he could only discern in it a principle of undisciplined subjectivity, which might endanger the orderly existence of the Church; in the place of it he put, therefore, the new *law of the Church*, which he most characteristically connected with the two models of the political and military organization of the Roman state and the sacerdotal hierarchy of the Jewish theocracy.[1] This was not an intentional concession of Heathen Christianity to Jewish Christians, or a conscious renunciation of Paulinism, the dogmatic form of which Clement, as we have seen, sedulously retains; it was, on the contrary, the insensible supplanting of the Pauline spirit of freedom and inward personal experience by a new spirit of legalism and external authority, for which Rome and Jerusalem offered their joint assistance. As a fact, the principle of authority represented by James thereby triumphed in the Church for nearly fifteen hundred years over the principle of liberty represented by Paul, but it was rendered possible

---

[1] Ep. I. ad Cor. xxxvii. xl.

simply because Rome succeeded to the heritage of Jerusalem; and Palestinian legalism having been stripped of its specifically Jewish form and invested with the Roman spirit of government, was made to serve the purposes of the universal Church. But the watchword in this fusion of Jewish and Roman characteristics was the name of *Peter*, the representative of historical tradition and of practical ecclesiastical moderation; in Clement's Epistle he is already placed before Paul, from whom he was destined subsequently to wrest the pre-eminence more and more completely.

The ultimate cause of this transformation of Paulinism into Catholicism was, it is true, to be found in the great historical fact of the migration of Christianity from Jerusalem to Rome, but it was materially assisted and accelerated by the conflicts provoked by heretical Gnosticism. The greater the dangers which threatened the Church from the phantastic mythology, the unhistorical docetism, and the inactive spiritualism of the Gnostics, the greater was the common interest of all moderate parties in the Church in putting down this enemy. And as the gnosis of Marcion, which originated in Paulinism, was the most dangerous from its importance and the heretical movement which it caused, the orthodox Paulinists were most immediately interested in rejecting every compromising connection with this hyper-Paulinism, and in maintaining as decidedly as possible their orthodox position in opposition to it. It is, however, implied in the nature of the case, and recurs in ecclesiastical conflicts of all ages, that the representatives of a principle are, in a contention with one of its radical extremes, often driven more or less from their original position and brought nearer to their earlier opponents : alarmed and vexed at the exaggeration and abuse of their own principle, they insensibly qualify and soften it down. And that this was the fate of orthodox Paulinism in its conflict with heretical Gnosticism, may be plainly seen in the Deutero-Pauline and Ignatian Epistles, which represent the increasing transformation of Paulinism into Catholicism during the second and third quarters of the second century.

The false teachers opposed in the Pastoral Epistles

are no other than the heretical Gnostics of the second century, and are in fact expressly described, 1 Tim. vi. 20, as professing "the Gnosis falsely so-called." Only it is not a particular system, or a specific Gnostic school, which is opposed; the Gnostic heresy as a whole, as a general tendency of the age, is made the subject of summary condemnation. In general the charge is brought against it of over-estimating the value of theoretical controversies and phantastic speculations at the cost of practical godliness and the harmony of the Church. Departures from the faith of the Church are, further, everywhere brought into intimate connection with corruption of the heart and moral errors; and the sketch of the false teachers presented, which is so gloomy in this respect, appears to combine even vices of an opposite nature, such as love of pleasure and sensual wantonness with scrupulous asceticism. It is hard to say whether, and to what extent, orthodox zeal may possibly have drawn a darker picture of the opponents than the fact justified. Of specific errors which are either expressly or allusively combated the following may be mentioned: a spiritualistic denial of the resurrection, dualistic asceticism, mythological genealogies, i.e. the doctrine of *æons*, the Marcionite antithesis of Law and Gospel, of a Creator and a Redeemer, Gnostic particularism, and a Docetic Christology; [1] the latter, which appears to be but slightly alluded to, has become the subject of lengthy controversy in the somewhat later Ignatian Epistles.

The authors of the Deutero-Pauline and the Ignatian Epistles did not propose as their object a refutation of the Gnostic heresies or a dogmatic discussion with their upholders; they simply confronted them with " sound doctrine according to godliness," i.e. the consensus of opinion in the Church generally, putting forward the tradition of the Church, as the truth, in correction of their errors. The familiar antithesis of orthodoxy and heterodoxy appears here for the first time: the truth is whatever is believed by the Church and is based upon its traditions; error is whatever departs from the general belief

---

[1] 2 Tim. ii. 18 ; Tit. i. 14 sq. ; 1 Tim. i. 4, 7, 17, ii. 4, 5, 6, iii. 16, iv. 3, 7, 10, vi. 4, 5, 16, 20.

and tradition of the community. One natural consequence of this principle of authority is that faith, which in Paul's view had been the subjective act of the surrender of the heart to Christ, acquires now a completely objective, dogmatic significance: it is sometimes soundness of belief, or submission to the form of teaching sanctioned by the Church; at others it is really identified with that teaching, becoming thus doctrinal belief[1] (*fides quæ creditur*), which already begins to be definitively fixed in formulæ as a *regula fidei*, after the manner of the creeds.[2] From this follows, as a further necessary consequence, that inasmuch as faith consists simply in a dogmatic assent to the doctrine of the Church, it can no longer of itself bring justification, but requires to be supplemented by love and other virtues;[3] further, that though at first the meritoriousness of " good works" is denied,[4] they acquire

---

[1] 1 Tim. i. 4, 5, 19, ii. 7, iii. 9, iv. 1, 6, vi. 10, 21 ; Tit. i. 4.

[2] 1 Tim. iii. 16.

[3] 1 Tim. ii. 15, iv. 12, vi. 11 ; 2 Tim. ii. 22, iii. 10 ; Tit. ii. 2.

[4] Tit. iii. 5 sq.

ever greater significance and value, so that the first
Epistle to Timothy is able to see in them a good
foundation and degree of salvation.[1] As the primitive Pauline antithesis of faith and works has been
thereby rendered meaningless, so the previous cardinal point of controversy between Paulinism and
Judaism—the religious question as to the validity
of the Law—has lost its interest when looked at
from the standpoint of the Paulinism of the Church,
and is simply treated as settled by the moral
principle that the Law is necessary for the wicked
but superfluous for the good.[2] Of the law of the
spirit, however, which Paul had put in opposition
to the law of the letter, not a word is now said.
On the other hand, the Church is thrust the more
prominently forward as "the pillar and basis of the
truth," "the firm foundation of God," upon which
the existence of Christianity as well as the salvation of individuals rests.[3] Paul had declared that
Jesus Christ alone was the foundation laid for all;

---

[1] 1 Tim. iii. 13, vi. 18, ii. 15.   [2] 1 Tim. i. 7 sq.

[3] 1 Tim. iii. 15; 2 Tim. ii. 19.

the Epistle to the Ephesians had added Apostles
and Prophets; but now the Church is, without any
reservation, made the foundation. And the Church
derives its unity and stability no longer from the
free spirit of the sons of God animating all its
members equally, but from ecclesiastical offices, consecrated by special spiritual endowment, imparted
by the sacramental ceremony of ordination. The
constitution of the Church appears in the First
Epistle to Timothy, the latest of the Deutero-Pauline
Epistles, as already at that stage of development
in which not only the Elders, or Presbyters, have
formed themselves into a closed college, but the
monarchical head of the Bishop begins already to
rise from their midst; with the imposition of the
hands of the Presbytery the charisma of the office
is communicated to him (Timothy is meant to
represent the Bishop).[1] Upon the Bishop rests the
obligation to see that sound doctrine is maintained
against heretical teachers; he also exercises discipline over the Presbyters; he has authority to

---

[1] 1 Tim. iv. 14.

grant or to refuse (to sinners and the fallen) admission into the Church by the imposition of his hands.[1]

If in this last of the Letters written in Paul's name the evident aim appears to give the Church stability by means of organized ecclesiastical offices, and especially the Episcopate, a glance at the Epistles published in the honoured name of the martyr *Ignatius* by a later Paulinist enables us to see with what increased energy and success within a few years that endeavour to strengthen ecclesiastical authority by means of the Episcopate was prosecuted amid the Church's struggles with domestic and foreign foes. While in the first Epistle of Timothy we observe only the growing desire to distinguish the Bishop from the Presbyters, the distinction is an accomplished fact in the Ignatian Epistles. The Bishop is no longer *primus inter pares*, but his relation to the Presbyters is like that of God or Christ, whose place he occupies, to the Apostles, whose college is perpetuated in the col-

---

[1] 1 Tim. i. 3, 18, iv. 6, ii. 16, v. 19, 20, 22.

lege of the Presbyters. The title to ecclesiastical offices is based on direct appointment to them by Christ and endowment with the Holy Spirit. The Bishop is the shepherd, under whose care alone the sheep are safe from the wolves (heretical teachers). Only they who go with the Bishop and the Presbyters can belong to God and Christ, for apart from them there is no Church. As Christ did nothing without the Father, so Christians ought to do nothing without the Bishops and Presbyters. He that honours the Bishop is honoured of God; he that does anything without the Bishop serves the Devil and defiles his conscience. No eucharist, baptism, or even marriage, is well-pleasing to God without the sanction of the Bishop.[1] Thus distinctly has the principle of the genuine Catholic hierarchy already reached a fully developed form: ecclesiastical offices intervene between God and man; on the relation of the believer to the priest depend his relation to God, the purity of his

---

[1] Ignat. *ad Magn.* vi. vii. ; *Trall.* iii. vii. ; *Philad.* i.—iii. ; *Smyrn.* viii. ix. ; *Polycarp,* v.

conscience, the acceptability of his worship and his moral action, the determination of his salvation or condemnation! Still—what is most remarkable of all—with all this, pseudo-Ignatius claims to be a good Paulinist; with the rigour of a Marcion he combats adherence to the Jewish Law as infatuation and wickedness, and, in opposition to Judaism, places, as the one inviolable authority of Christians, Jesus Christ, and his cross, and his death, and faith, by which he seeks to receive justification.[1] We perceive from this that while Catholicism retained the dogmatic form of Paulinism and continued to protest against the positive form of the Jewish Law, it substituted at the same time for the spirit of Paulinism the Jewish spirit of Legalism, for which the foundations of a strong citadel in the Roman Church were now laid in the new form of the legalistic system of ecclesiastical Catholicism.

No advance was made beyond this position throughout the Middle Ages. Nor was the theology of the great Church Father *Augustine* so

---

[1] Ignat. *ad Philad.* viii.

much a revival of Paulinism as a most thorough-
going transformation of it into ecclesiastical Catholicism.   Undoubtedly Augustine's nature had very
close affinity to that of Paul, but in him we have
the evangelical Paul Romanized.   He shares Paul's
profound sense of dependence on God, of the unconditionality of the Divine grace, without which he
felt himself to be as powerless for good as he was
wretched and reprobate.   He had also experienced
in his own history the tremendous contrariety of
sin and grace, and had himself gone through the
terrible conflict of the flesh and the spirit; after
manifold errors in thought and life, in complete
doubt of finding the truth and in despair of attaining to goodness, he had experienced in his own
person the saving power of the gospel of the grace
of God in Christ.   And when once he had been
taken possession of by this truth, Augustine made it,
with the decisive thoroughness of strong natures
such as his, the one absorbing idea of his whole life.
As Paul had felt himself and the whole world crucified with Christ, and was thenceforth determined to
know nothing else save Jesus Christ as crucified,

so Augustine, after his violent break with his past life, regarded everything belonging to natural humanity as worthless in comparison with the sole source of truth and goodness which had been opened up to him in the grace of Christ.

Sin and grace, these two poles of Pauline theology, were likewise the axes of the religious feeling and the theological thought of Augustine. And he, too, traced the roots of this antithesis, which he had experienced in the first instance in his own life, back to the beginning of the world's history, and, in fact, beyond the world into the mysterious darkness of the eternal decrees of Deity. If sin is such a terrible power as Augustine perceived it to be, a victory over which is more than man's strength is sufficient for, and can be gained by the grace of God alone, it cannot comprise merely the separate and casual deeds of individuals, but it is, as Augustine teaches with Paul, a universal despotic power, holding the entire race captive under its resistless sway, a fatal calamity inflicted on mankind. But since this moral condition cannot have been originally created by God, Augustine looks upon it as the consequence of human guilt, as a punishment inflicted upon the whole human race for Adam's first offence. In these general ideas Augustine is at one with Paul; but in his further development of the consequences of the Fall, he goes far beyond his predecessor. According to his view, after the Fall the entire human race has become altogether a *massa perditionis*, absolutely ruled by ungodly selfishness and sensual desires, free only to do evil, without any power to do good, so that even the virtues of the Heathen are but splendid vices. If with this excessively pessimistic estimate of the actual condition of mankind, Augustine has already gone far beyond Paul, this is still more the case when he teaches the transference of the guilt of Adam to the race in such a manner that even infants are doomed to eternal damnation in hell simply on account of original sin, as far as they are not saved by grace through baptism. In support of this cruel theory, Augustine appeals to Rom. v. 12, a passage which really teaches nothing of the kind, Paul's argument being simply that with the universaiity of sin physical death likewise

extended to all men, because all (personally) sinned
—an argument, therefore, which actually excludes
the Augustinian doctrine of original sin. Augustine
completely twisted the meaning of this passage by
the false translation, *in quo omnes peccaverunt*, and
his inference therefrom that, on the ground of
their being virtually included in their first parent,
all men shared his sin and are justly condemned
on that account. The foundation of this strange
theory is not, however, to be found merely in a
misunderstood passage of Scripture ; the falsely
interpreted text only served Augustine as the sub-
struction of a theory previously adopted, the real
reasons for which must be sought, firstly, in the
depth and intensity of his sense of sin—a consequence not less of his temperament than of his personal history ; secondly, however, and chiefly, in
ecclesiastical motives, namely, the demonstration of
the absolute necessity of the Church's means of
grace, particularly baptism.

And this is the point where the Augustinian
theory deviates furthest from the Pauline. According to Paul, grace was the love of God revealed in

Christ, which, made known through the Gospel, apprehended by faith and borne witness to in the heart by the holy spirit of adoption, unites the believer *directly* with God, and thereby delivers him from all human thraldom. Augustine, on the contrary, conceives of grace as so completely restricted to the channel of the sacramental ceremonies of the Church—and of the Roman Catholic Church represented by the clergy—that salvation, as well as the moral worth of men, is made to depend unconditionally on membership in this Church and obedience to its authority. As Augustine maintains, everything may be had outside the Church save salvation; and although a man supposes he leads a good life, he will nevertheless, for the one crime of separation from the Church, not obtain salvation, but the wrath of God remains upon him. According to Augustine, the Church is so exclusively in possession of the whole truth, human reason is since the Fall so totally depraved, that all criticism of the doctrine of the Church is from the very first quite out of the question, and nothing remains for us but an unconditional subjection to its authority, as professedly rendered sacred by Apostolic tradition. And since the Church is identified with the *civitas Dei*, which is destined in the Divine counsels to triumph over the states of the world, she extends her royal prerogative over the entire life of Christians; secular institutions receive from her their divine sanction and moral worth; the State is especially under the obligation to lend its strong arm to her for the punishment and subjugation of her enemies—*cogite intrare !* By his calamitous misinterpretation of this passage of Scripture with reference to the employment of the compulsory power of the State, in reply to the Donatists, Augustine laid the foundation of the enthralment of men's minds for a thousand years to the hierarchy, a condition the most direct opposite of the freedom of the children of God to which we are called according to Paul's gospel.

This ecclesiastical slavery is further promoted in Augustine's system by that aspect of the doctrine of grace which was intended in Paul's thought to constitute the firmest support of personal religious assurance and freedom—the doctrine of predestina-

tion. Paul had based the assurance of Christians,
with its superiority to all the vicissitudes of the
world and time, on the fact that they are conscious
of being the objects of a Divine love which infalli-
bly brings those whom it has once chosen and pre-
destined to salvation to the destination of heavenly
blessedness (Rom. viii. 29, 30). The idea of predestination is here nothing else than the theological
expression of the immediate religious consciousness
of enjoying the favour of God, a consciousness
which derives its certainty from the witness of the
Spirit felt within the heart (viii. 16), and for that
reason involves deliverance from all fear of the
world and man, for "if God is for us, who can be
against us?" (viii. 31). But in Augustine's system,
the idea of predestination is intended, on the contrary, to serve the purpose of keeping the Christian in perpetual uncertainty as to his salvation,
of damping the happy assurance (or "pride," as
Augustine terms it) of the possession of the Divine
favour, and of compelling him, as thus deprived of
all inward support, to take refuge in the ecclesiastical ordinances of salvation. As, according to

Augustine, grace is applied only externally by the agency of ecclesiastical functions, and has not its roots in our own inner being or its channel in our personal volition (which, indeed, is in his view free only to choose the evil), it cannot truly enter into our proper nature so as to become our own actual life, but remains an incomprehensible mystery, hidden in the Divine counsels, before which we can only prostrate ourselves in awful fear and resignation. This is the habit of thought of Catholic Christianity. According to it men cling to the mediation of the Church, because they are unable to find God in their own souls, or to hear within their own hearts His infallible revelations; they must try to gain salvation by external works according to the direction of the Church, because they are unable to obtain it by the inward action of personal surrender to God. Thus the religion of the Spirit is converted into a system of ceremonial observances.

At the same time, the Augustinian doctrine of predestination, the roots of which were in Paulinism, retained all along an element of affinity to the latter, and might therefore, under favourable conditions, some day conduct to a position the exact opposite of ecclesiastical Augustinianism. According to Augustine, the doctrine of predestination was meant to keep men in uncertainty as to their salvation and thereby in a condition of dependence on the Church. But suppose the devout soul in its feeling of the love of God has become conscious of its election, must not this very consciousness serve to liberate it from dependence on the Church? Will not the function of the Church as the channel of salvation lose its value and importance in proportion as stress is laid on personal experience of Divine grace, which, in more profoundly religious natures particularly, is usually combined with the immediate certainty of its being a living reality? For this reason we need not be surprised that the more profound and independent religious spirits of later times took the Augustinian doctrines of grace as their starting-point, and used them as a means of delivering themselves from the ban of the Augustinian doctrine of the Church, and of a return, beyond Catholicism, to Paulinism and its gospel of the freedom of the sons of God.

This was done for the first time in a thorough manner by the bold Oxford reformer, *John Wiclif,* who converted the Pauline and Augustinian doctrine of predestination into a battering-ram for shaking the very foundation of the Catholic system—priestly absolution. One of his most important principles was, that neither the Pope, nor even the Lord Jesus Christ, can grant dispensation or indulgence otherwise than as the Deity has determined from all eternity by righteous decree; furthermore, that it is blasphemous to maintain that deserts can, like accidental predicates, be transferred from one subject to another, a supposition upon which the Catholic doctrine of a *thesaurus* of supererogatory merits, and its administration by the clergy, is founded. Wiclif energetically exhorts the soldiers of Christ to reject such fictions of the Prince of darkness, which only serve to befool the Church, and to put on Jesus Christ.[1] Huss took up Wiclif's ideas again. Starting from the conception of the Church as the collective body of the predestinated, he drew the inference that Papal indulgences were of uncertain value, since

---

[1] Trialogus, iv. 32.

it could not be known of any man, not even of the Pope himself, whether he belonged to the number of the predestinated or not, and whether his indulgences were in conformity with or opposed to the eternal decrees of God.   As Paul had proved the invalidity of the Law by means of the Law, so ecclesiastical Augustinianism is assailed by Wiclif and Huss with Augustine's weapons.   Generally speaking, it is true that controversies of this class are too exclusively occupied with scholastic abstractions, and the use made of the doctrine of predestination is confined too much to the region of theological dogma, and has too little intimate connection with the inner religious consciousness, to exert a quickening and renewing influence upon the hearts of the people.

It was *Luther* in whom the spirit of Paulinism first re-appeared in all its power, successfully bursting the fetters of Catholicism, by which it had been held bound for fourteen hundred years.   How may men get rid of their sins and be righteous?   This cardinal point of the doctrine of Paul was the burning question of Luther's life, the settlement of which he had vainly sought in the ecclesiastical religion of works, and at length, like Paul, found in faith in Christ the Reconciler. It was not, as in the case of Augustine, grievous sins of unrestrained passion which oppressed Luther's conscience; his life had been as blameless, according to human judgment, as Paul's pre-Christian life under the Law. What drove Luther into a monastery, and tormented him there amid all his monastic exercises, was the burning desire of his devout heart for peace and reconciliation with God, which, do what he might, was perpetually frustrated by the profound feeling of his tender conscience that the chasm between the holy God and sinful man could not be got over by any resolves and efforts on his part. As Luther had experienced in himself more deeply than any one else since Paul the insufficiency of his own righteousness, he likewise made righteousness by faith the watchword of his life more absolutely than any one after Paul. And, unlike Augustine, Luther did not conceive justifying grace as exclusively connected with the agency of the visible Church and her sacerdotal functions, but, like Paul, beheld it directly in Christ as the reflection of the Divine love, and therefore embraced it directly by faith in Christ; in the surrender of his heart to the Saviour he became so immediately assured of the love of God and of peace with Him, that nothing could any more come to separate him and his God. In Luther's view, therefore, grace is no longer, as in Augustine's, a blessing deposited in the Church only, and, in relation to the consciousness of the individual, something always external and accordingly problematic, but manifests itself as the inward experience of the human soul, as its own new spirit of adoption. But where the spirit of the Lord is, there is liberty. Therefore grace, which, according to Augustine, enchained men to the Church, became for Luther the hammer with which he broke in pieces all such human fetters and triumphantly recovered the lost freedom of the Christian man. The word of Paul to the Galatians, "For freedom Christ has made us free; stand fast, therefore, and be not entangled again in a yoke of bondage!" was first understood again in its full significance by Luther, and proclaimed to enslaved

Christendom as the message of Divine deliverance.
At this trumpet-blast all the walls of that spiritual
dungeon fell, by means of which the Romish hierarchy had set up and established its sway over
men's consciences and the life of society. The wall
of separation between the clergy and the laity
disappeared before the general priesthood of all
believers; the tyranny over consciences exercised
in the confessional was broken by the free access of
all believers to the grace wherein we stand; the
gates of the monasteries were thrown open and
their captives set free, and parsonages grew up and
became the consecrated scenes of godly family bliss
and pure manners, as models and sources of blessing
to countless numbers.

And it is at this point where Luther advanced
not merely beyond Augustine, but beyond Paul
also, or rather that he carried out the Pauline
principle, "all things are yours," more thoroughly
than the Apostle himself. For Paul the world had
been crucified in Christ, not merely in the sense
that sinful worldly desires had lost their charm for
him, but also in the sense that the social life of the

earth seemed to be without value and importance in view of the immediate appearance of the celestial Christ, to which the eager hope of all Christians was directed. The time, Paul says, is short; therefore they who have wives must be as though they had none, and it is better to remain unmarried, to be in readiness for the coming Lord. This early Christian contrast between the present world and the expected Messianic kingdom became subsequently in Catholicism an opposition between the world and the Church, and secular and spiritual life,—an opposition which was not less prejudicial to the true appreciation of ordinary natural life than favourable to the despotic rule of society by the hierarchy. Luther was the first to get rid of this dualism, which dominated the whole of Christendom down to his time, and to recognize the moral life of Christians as one harmonious whole, that is, as the organic development of faith working by love. Everything that proceeds from this motive, not excepting labour in the humblest vocation, is also well-pleasing to God, a true act of worship of positive value, and indeed of much higher value than the unproductive ascetic life of the clergy. The married state particularly is in Luther's estimation so far from being merely a concession to human weakness, and a lower state than the unmarried, as the Catholic Church had taught with Paul and Augustine, that, on the contrary, it "ought a hundred times more justly to be called spiritual than the monastic state," for it is an excellent means of educating man in faith, patience and humility, for practising obedience in the fulfilment of daily duties, and in the joint bearing of the cross. Thus it was by Luther that the kingdom of Christ was for the first time transferred from an anti-natural transcendental world—whether eschatological or ecclesiastical—into the natural world of the present earthly life, and thus made the guiding and moralizing power in all spheres of human existence. It was thereby that the saying of Jesus regarding the leaven and the mustard-seed was completely fulfilled, and the utterance of Paul, "The kingdom of God is righteousness and peace and joy in the Holy Spirit: whoever serveth Christ herein is well-pleasing to God and approved of men" (Rom. xiv. 17).

While, however, Luther unquestionably carried
out the ethical side of the Pauline principle more
completely than Paul himself, as respects its theological side he did not advance beyond the doctrinal system which proceeded from Paulinism and
was afterwards mixed with Augustinian, Anselmian
and other medieval elements.   With Augustine he
teaches the total depravity of mankind through
Adam's Fall, the want of all freedom in the human
will to choose the good, the damnation of all the
unbaptized on account of original sin, and the
necessity of the baptism of infants for salvation, a
belief which can hardly be made to accord with his
Pauline doctrine of justification by faith.   And,
going beyond Augustine even, he taught the real
presence of the body of Christ in the sacrament of
the Lord's Supper, and in conjunction therewith
the ubiquity of Christ in his human combined with
the divine nature, of which there is as little to be
found in Paul's writings as of the Athanasian doctrine of the Trinity, which Luther likewise maintained as an article of faith.   In his doctrine of the
Atonement he followed Anselm, who had given a

coarser form to the Pauline theory of expiation in
the sense of the Catholic doctrine of the supererogatory and transferable merits of the saints; but the
very theory of the meritorious satisfaction of Christ,
which was in Anselm's system both a natural consequence and again a confirmation of the merits of
the saints and the Church, was used by Luther,
on the contrary, to set aside the merits of the
saints and the whole system of meritorious works.
He sought accordingly to refute the Catholic idea of
righteousness by works from the position of the
Catholic doctrine of Atonement, just as Paul had set
aside the religion of the Law from the standpoint
of the Law.   In neither case are we able to call in
question the propriety, or indeed the historical
necessity, of such a line of procedure; at the same
time we cannot shut our eyes to the great difficulties which arise for thoughtful minds from this
employment of conceptions belonging peculiarly
to the antiquated standpoint in establishing and
formulating the truth of the new principle.   The
contradictions and theoretical stumbling-blocks
which are the inevitable consequences of this line

of procedure were probably felt more painfully by Luther than by Paul; for that very reason he repudiated more rudely than almost any one before his day the right of the reason to judge critically in matters of faith, and demanded its unconditional submission to the authority of the sacred Scriptures. The difficulty, however, was not thus got over, but only increased; for his own action was in real and marked contradiction to his principle of the repudiation of the reason and its right of free inquiry. Not only had he accorded to sound reason the amplest scope in his polemic with Catholic traditions, but he bowed to the authority of the word of Scripture only so far as it harmonized with his own religious convictions; when that was not the case, he did not scruple himself, it is well known, to pass the freest opinions, not only upon points of detail, but also upon entire books of the Bible. In fact, in this respect Luther followed in the footsteps of Paul, inasmuch as the latter likewise acknowledged *in thesi* the literal authority of the word of God as written in the Law, but *in praxi* took the greatest liberties in his application and interpretation of the written word

in favour of his own Christian view of the abrogation of the Law.   Common to both religious heroes
was, therefore, the limitation imposed upon them
by their historical position, that they could give
didactic expression to the independent truth of
which they were the original discoverers only
through the inadequate and perishable forms of a
traditional theology, by the normal authority of
which they still felt themselves bound, whilst as
regards the contents of their faith they had advanced
beyond it : their treasure of divine truth they possessed in earthen vessels.   It appears, however, to
be the tragical lot of mankind, that of the great
performances of their historical heroes it is always
the limited and transient form rather than the eternal
ideal substance which in the first instance receives
chief attention.   As we saw above that in ecclesiastical Catholicism the dogmatic form of Paulinism
was preserved deprived of its evangelical spirit, so
at the Reformation a similar fate befel revived
Paulinism in the new scholasticism of orthodox
Protestantism.

There was in this respect, however, an essential
difference.   When once the Pauline principle of

unfettered and inward faith had been put into the
centre of the theology of the Church, it could not
be again pushed aside ; the Protestant Christian
could not wholly renounce his right to derive
the gospel directly from its first source indepen-
dently of all ecclesiastical and traditional formularies
and ordinances, and to test all outward testimonies
by the inward witness of the Spirit of God. In
proportion as the wants of the religious heart
remained unsupplied by the cold formalism of
dogmatic theology, and the intellect was vainly tor-
tured in the effort to remove its contradictions, the
more necessary in the interest of both was the
reaction of the free Protestant spirit against the
new ecclesiastical Law. This reaction took place
in the form of German Pietism and English Methodism in response to emotional needs, and in the form
of English Deism and German Rationalism to meet
the necessities of the reason. The relation these
movements held to Paulinism was various. While
Methodism and Pietism (particularly of the Mora-
vian Brethren) found in Pauline mystical faith and
love of the Saviour a healing and rejuvenating spring
for the paralyzed religious life, Rationalism for the

most part took too great offence at the dogmatic in-
tegument of Paulinism in the coarse form of orthodox
teaching, to be able to devote to it unprejudiced
attention.   Still noteworthy exceptions were not
altogether wanting, amongst whom we may discover
the predecessors of the modern Tübingen school.
To their number belongs especially the English
Freethinker *Thomas Morgan*, who is entitled to the
honour of being the first since Marcion's time
to perceive the profound difference between the
legalistic national Jewish Christianity of the earlier
Apostles and the universalistic Christianity of Paul,
and to insist emphatically on the originality of the
latter.   He extols Paul as "the great free-thinker
of his age, and the brave defender of Reason against
Authority," who as a solitary man, in the long
conflict with the Jewish and Jewish-Christian opposition, steadily maintained his position and never
admitted the religious obligation of the Mosaic Law.[1]
Morgan also made numerous and excellent observa-

---

[1] In his "Moral Philosopher, in a Dialogue betweeen Phila-
lethes, a Christian Deist, and Theophanes, a Christian Jew"
(1737—1740).   Comp. the interesting article of David Patrick
in the *Theological Review*, Oct. 1877, pp. 562 sq.

tions on the gradual fusion of the two hostile parties
in the unity of the Catholic Church, on the effects
of Jewish Christianity traceable in the hierarchical
character of that Church, on the Roman legend of
Peter, and on the strength acquired by the Episcopate
in the struggle with Gnosticism.　It cannot, however, be denied that Morgan suffered himself to be
misled by his sympathy with the Apostle of freedom
so as to make him too much like a modern, and in
attention to the anti-Judaic to overlook the Jewish
features of Paul's thought; still the boldness and
sagacity of his critical observations, which were
a century in advance of his time, deserve every
acknowledgment.　Whilst the criticism of Morgan
is based rather upon bold intuition than exact
exegetical and historical inquiry, *Semler*, the
" Father of German Rationalism," was the first
to apply the method of historical criticism to the
study of the Bible, and by its means to quicken
the sight for the discovery of the exact differences
between the primitive Christian parties; yet his
hints attracted for a long time but little notice.　It
was the great scholar *Ferdinand Christian Baur*,

distinguished equally for his learning, his critical
acumen and his constructive genius, who first succeeded in for ever scattering the thick mists of
traditional illusion which had settled over the
early years of our religion, and in obtaining a
connected and critically established view of the
actual development of primitive Christianity, and
especially of the decisive part Paul took therein.
However much there may be in the results of his
labours to correct in detail, at all events they supply
the solid groundwork upon which the scientific examination of primitive Christianity has been since
building.

I have now reached the conclusion of the historical task proposed to me.   History, however, ought
to be an instructress helping us to understand the
present and the future.   For that reason, you may
justly look for an answer to the question, What significance has Paulinism with regard to the development of Christianity in the present and future ? On
this question I can give my view with the greater
brevity as the answer to it is really contained in
what has already been said.   We have repeatedly

seen that wherever the spirit of Paulinism made itself felt, it was an influence bringing freedom and inward depth to the religious life, delivering men from all externalities, and uniting them directly with God : this constitutes the specifically Christian and permanent element of Paulinism. But we have also seen that from the very first Paulinism assumed a dogmatic form, which, taken in the first instance from Jewish elements and afterwards extended and developed into a dogmatic system by Alexandrine Gnosticism, was constituted by the Church an obligatory law of belief and tended growingly to become an impeding fetter and an oppressive yoke to the religious spirit : this forms the frail earthen vessel containing the precious treasure of the Pauline gospel.   The dissimilarity which has from the very first until now marked the views taken of Paulinism is explained by this two-fold aspect of it.   Some looked mainly at its valuable religious contents, and on their account regarded its dogmatic form as an inalienable truth invested with binding authority, but they thereby perverted the Pauline gospel of the freedom of the sons of God into an enslaving letter. Others, on the contrary, took the greater offence at this perishable form the more it was pressed upon them with the claim of possessing infallible and indisputable authority; and being unable to distinguish between it and its spiritual contents, they rejected Paulinism altogether, and demanded a return to Christianity anterior to Paul, while their conception of the latter was nevertheless unconsciously influenced by the idealizing spirit of Paulinism. From both these mistakes a critical and historical study of the Bible may preserve us, teaching us, as it does, to distinguish between the spirit and the letter, the permanent and the transient. The more fully this distinction is made a part of the general consciousness of theologians and churches, the easier will it be for the Church of the present age to accomplish a perpetual reformation of its forms of doctrine by means of the spirit of Paulinism.

In the performance of this pressing task, we may take the Apostle Paul himself as our model. As he treated the words of the Old Testament, notwithstanding his great reverence of it, with the supreme freedom of the religious spirit, which is convinced

that the truth inwardly revealed to it must be likewise the deepest meaning and true significance of
every historical revelation, hidden indeed from
the view of ordinary men, but disclosed to the
more penetrating glance of the spiritual man (2 Cor.
iii. 6—17), so we on the same principle may adopt
the same line of procedure with regard to the letter
of the Pauline and the ecclesiastical systems of
doctrine.   Since we have learnt from Paul that
Christ has called us to freedom, and that the
spiritual man has the right and the duty to judge
and to prove all things,[1] we will not put ourselves
again under the servile yoke of the letter, which
has binding authority for those under age only,
and not for the free sons of God.   On the other
hand, as we know that all things are lawful for
us but all things are not expedient, and that
knowledge puffeth up but love edifieth,[2] we will
not with violent hands precipitately break up or
cast away the forms in which the Apostles and
Prophets deposited for Christendom the religious

---

[1] 1 Cor. ii. 15 ; 1 Thess. v. 21.   [2] 1 Cor. vi. 12, viii. 1.

U

treasure of the gospel, forms in which the founders
of our Protestant churches confessed their faith, and
to which the hearts of countless numbers of Christians are still deeply attached. What should prevent
us from interpreting and applying the dogmas,
which can no longer be appropriated by us in their
literal meaning, as valuable symbols of religious and
moral truths? Suppose, for instance, we find it
difficult to harmonize the doctrine of Adam's Fall
and Christ's Atonement with our ideas of the development of mankind and the educating revelation
of God. What should prevent our interpreting these
doctrines as symbols of the two opposing powers
the struggle of which extends through the entire
human race—the selfish love of the natural man,
which is the root of all evil, and the self-denying
love of man in the image of God, which procures
the weal of all by unselfish sacrifice, and by lowly
service obtains triumphant dominion? Or if, perhaps, we feel it difficult to harmonize the idea of a
personal descent of Christ from heaven, in the past
or in the future, with our conception of the universe and man, what can forbid us to find therein

the symbol of the elevated truth, that the ideal of man as the child of God had its eternal ground in the will of God, and was embodied in the fulness of time in Jesus Christ as the first-born among many brethren, whilst it is also being continually embodied in all those who embrace it in faith and make it a living reality in their hearts and lives? Would our Christian faith in the revelation of the Son of God in the flesh lose any of its elevating power if we conceived the miracle of the Incarnation as not confined to the solitary past appearance of Jesus on the earth, but understood it of the perpetual revelation of the Divine Spirit in the miraculous transformation of men from sinful children of Adam into holy children of God? Or need our hope of Christ's second coming lose any of its consoling virtue if we no longer looked upon it as a single marvellous future event of which we are hardly competent to form any conception, but understood it as a symbol of the universal destination of humanity to grow into the unity of the "body of Christ," that is, the organic association of the children of God, who are animated by the one spirit of the love of

God, in whose midst, therefore, the Lord, who is spirit, is always occupied in his triumphant coming?

But enough of these examples: which are intended only to indicate how everywhere the letter of Pauline and ecclesiastical theology may be regarded as the transparent covering of sublime truths, which it is our just right and our sacred duty more and more clearly to discover, to bring forth in ever greater purity, and to use with increasing freedom for the edification of our modern Christian churches. For the letter killeth, but the spirit giveth life.